C000202547

TENA ŠTIVIČIĆ

Tena Štivičić's plays *Can't*
Two of Us, *Fragile!*, *Fireflies*, *Felix*, *Invisible*, *Europa*, and
plays for children, *Perceval – the Quest for the Grail*, and *Psst*
have been performed in a number of European countries and
translated and published in ten languages. They have won
numerous awards including the European Author's Award and
the Innovation Award at Heidelberg Stückemarkt for *Fragile!*

In 2007, she wrote a one-act play for Goldoni Terminus, a
collection of short plays commissioned to celebrate the three
hundredth anniversary of Goldoni's birth, which premiered at the
Venice Biennale. She is a columnist for *Zaposlena* magazine in
Croatia and has published two books of her columns. Her play
Seven Days in Zagreb was the Croatian partner in the ETC Orient
Express international project in summer 2009. *Europa* was
co-written with Malgorzata Sikorska Miszczuk, Lutz Hübner and
Steve Waters for the Birmingham Rep, ZKM Zagreb, Teatr Polski
Bydgoszcz and Dresden Staatstheater. A feature film adapted
from her play *Invisible* is currently in pre-production.

Other Titles in this Series

Tena Štivičić

3 WINTERS

NICK HERN BOOKS

London

www.nickhernbooks.co.uk

A Nick Hern Book

3 Winters first published in Great Britain in 2014 as a paperback original by Nick Hern Books Limited, The Glasshouse, 49a Goldhawk Road, London W12 8QP

3 Winters copyright © 2014 Tena Štivičić

Tena Štivičić has asserted her moral right to be identified as the author of this work

Cover image by Jagoda Kaloper-Tajder

Designed and typeset by Nick Hern Books, London
Printed in Great Britain by CPI Group (UK) Ltd

A CIP catalogue record for this book is available from the British Library

ISBN 978 1 84842 449 4

MIX
Paper from
responsible sources
FSC
www.fsc.org   FSC® C013604

3 Winters was first performed in the Lyttelton auditorium of the National Theatre, London, on 3 December 2014 (previews from 26 November). The cast was as follows:

LUCIJA KOS (*1990*)	Charlotte Beaumont
DUNJA KING	Lucy Black
KAROLINA AMRUŠ (*1990*)	Susan Engel
MAŠA KOS	Siobhan Finneran
KARL DOLINAR	Daniel Flynn
KAROLINA AMRUŠ (*1945*)	Hermione Gulliford
ROSE KING	Jo Herbert
MARKO HORVAT (*1990*)	Alex Jordan
MARINKO/	Gerald Kyd
MARKO HORVAT (*2011*)	
ALEKSANDAR KING (*1990*)	James Laurenson
IGOR MALJEVIĆ	Jonny Magnanti
ALISA KOS (*2011*)	Jodie McNee
ALEKSANDAR KING (*1945*)	Alex Price
VLADO KOS	Adrian Rawlins
LUCIJA KOS (*2011*)	Sophie Rundle
ALISA KOS (*1990*)	Bebe Sanders
MONIKA ZIMA	Josie Walker

Director	Howard Davies
Designer	Tim Hatley
Lighting Designer	James Farncombe
Music	Dominic Muldowney
Projection Designer	Jon Driscoll for cineluma
Fight Director	Terry King
Sound Designer	Mike Walker
Staff Director	Melanie Hillyard
Company Voice Work	Kate Godfrey

For my mum,
and Nena
and Marija
and Monika

Characters

2011

ALISA KOS, *thirty-six*

LUCIJA KOS, *thirty-three, Alisa's sister*

MAŠA KOS, *sixty-six, Alisa and Lucija's mother*

VLADO (VLADIMIR) KOS, *sixty-seven, Alisa and Lucija's father*

DUNJA KING, *sixty-three, Maša's sister*

MARKO HORVAT, *thirty-nine, upstairs neighbour*

1990

MAŠA KOS, *forty-five*

VLADO KOS, *forty-six*

DUNJA KING (*married Dolinar*), *forty-two*

KARL DOLINAR, *forty-three, Dunja's husband*

KAROLINA AMRUŠ, *ninety-two, the original owner of the Kos house*

IGOR MALJEVIĆ, *forty-four, friend of the family*

ALEKSANDAR KING, *seventy-three, Dunja and Maša's father*

ALISA KOS, *fifteen*

LUCIJA KOS, *twelve*

MARKO HORVAT, *eighteen*

1945

ROSE KING, *twenty-seven*

ALEKSANDAR KING, *thirty*

MONIKA ZIMA, *forty-five*

KAROLINA AMRUŠ, *forty-seven*

MARINKO, *forty, a Communist official*

For a Guide to Pronunciation see page 109

Note on Play

Scene One takes place in an office. The rest of the play takes place in and around the Kos family house in Zagreb, Croatia. The Old Town is the historic core of Zagreb dating back to the twelfth century. The house was built and owned by the Amruš family, members of Zagreb aristocracy at the end of the nineteenth century. After the Second World War the house was nationalised and partitioned and has since been shared by at least three families at any given time. The Kos family lives in the central, biggest part of the house.

In between scenes we should see projections of the blueprints charting the changes in the layout of the house as well as projections of the Kos and Amruš family pictures throughout the last one hundred years.

This text went to press before the end of rehearsals and so may differ slightly from the play as performed.

Scene One

November, 1945.

Morning.

An office – plain – functional – Communist.

ROSE, *twenty-seven, stands in front of the desk. Her clothes are simple, clean and plain.* MARINKO, *a man in his forties, sits at the desk with a typewriter in front of him.*

MARINKO. Surname?

ROSE. King.

MARINKO. Name?

ROSE. Rose.

MARINKO. Married, unmarried, widowed?

ROSE. Married.

MARINKO. Maiden name?

ROSE. Zima.

MARINKO. Husband's surname?

ROSE. King.

MARINKO. Husband's name?

ROSE. Aleksandar.

   MARINKO *stops typing. He looks up.*

MARINKO. King, Aleksandar?

ROSE. He was born in 1918. Just before the unification. It was a popular name. The Prince Regent…

   MARINKO *eyes her suspiciously. He picks up the phone and dials.*

MARINKO. Let me speak to Goyko.

ROSE *shifts in her place. She looks around her.*

Goyko? Marinko. Listen, I've got a comrade here, last name King, first name Rose. Yes. She says the General sent her. To sort out the housing arrangements. Married, one child. Infant, born in the woods. They have nowhere to live. Yes. I'll wait.

He waits. Again, he eyes her. Top to bottom. She takes it in her stride. The waiting goes on for a long minute.

Yes? That's right. Understood.

He hangs up.

The General says I am to let you pick a key. Any key.

ROSE. I'm sorry?

MARINKO. Pick. A. House.

He signals over to another desk. There is a mountain of keys on it. A mountain.

She walks over to the keys. She picks up a few; an address is attached to each key. She reads the addresses.

ROSE. Whose houses are these, comrade?

MARINKO. They're ours.

ROSE. They're empty?

MARINKO. They're empty.

ROSE. And where are the people who lived in them?

MARINKO. Now, look here, comrade, enough with the questions. Pick a key, go get your child and your husband and start moving in.

ROSE *examines the keys, panicked. The clinking noise and* MARINKO's *gaze exacerbate her anxiety. The mountain of keys threatens to collapse and pour down on the floor.*

She focuses on one particular key.

She stares at it. She brings it over to MARINKO.

There we go. It wasn't that hard after all.

ROSE. No. I guess not.

> MARINKO *takes the key, opens a book to make a note. He looks at the address.*

MARINKO. Bourgeois taste, comrade.

> *She says nothing, quietly defying the accusation.*

Well, good luck to you. Death to fascism.

ROSE. Freedom to the people.

Scene Two

November, 2011.

It's early evening in the dining/living room of the Kos family. A typical room of an impoverished middle-class family. A few antique pieces. Some simple, jaded socialist items, a couple of new additions. A fancy CD player. A portrait of Karolina Amruš aged fifteen hangs on the wall; bright-red hair, a smart period dress from the early-twentieth century.

ALISA, thirty-six, and DUNJA, sixty-three, are at the table – looking over blueprints.

ALISA. This wall?

DUNJA. And this one. Except for the bathrooms, he wants everything to go back to how it was when the house was first built. Based on these original blueprints from 1898.

> VLADO, *sixty-seven, marches in – in through one door – followed by* LUCIJA, *thirty-three –*

VLADO. I'll be damned if I let a priest come into this house and lecture me.

LUCIJA. Dad –

VLADO. I agreed to attend the ceremony and grit my teeth in silence, but I will not eat the wafer, I will not pray and if anyone so much as thinks of having the house blessed –

LUCIJA. There will be no house blessings. But if the priest offers you the wafer, how hard would it be to take it? It's like a crisp. You like crisps.

– And he marches out through the other door. LUCIJA *follows him.*

ALISA. Isn't one supposed to be christened to have a church wedding?

MAŠA, *sixty-six, comes in carrying cutlery. She wears an apron over her clothes. She is a woman always in motion.*

MAŠA. Vlado! Lucija! Supper's ready. I am not going to tell you again.

DUNJA (*to* ALISA). She was christened two months ago.

ALISA *is stunned.* VLADO *comes in, foaming at the mouth, followed by* LUCIJA.

VLADO. It's when you think the worry days are over, you get through the childhood diseases, the grades, the coming-of-age, the drugs, the alcohol, the unsuitable boyfriends, all that and then they strike the final blow.

LUCIJA. Ah, Dad, pipe down.

MAŠA (*en passant*). Vlado, do give it a rest.

VLADO. Give it a rest? Give it a –

But MAŠA *has dashed off to the kitchen again.*

ALISA. Let's just sit down and have dinner, shall we?

Muttering under his breath, VLADO *goes to the table.* MAŠA *brings another bowl to the table.* DUNJA *lights a cigarette.*

MAŠA. Dunja, you're not going to smoke now?

DUNJA. I wasn't sure how long it was going to take.

VLADO (*to* MAŠA). It's you we're waiting for.

DUNJA *puts the cigarette out.*

MAŠA. Well, excuse me…

VLADO. What I mean is –

MAŠA. Because there was no reason whatsoever you couldn't have set the table.

VLADO. You could have asked –

MAŠA. I have been cooking supper for a whole legion of you for over thirty-five years. That is – (*Pauses to count.*) times five… Plus one when Dad was alive…

DUNJA. Twelve thousand give or take.

MAŠA. Twelve thousand suppers. Alongside raising children and working full time. And in those thirty-five years you have not been able to memorise that each day at suppertime the table needs setting.

VLADO. Bloody hell, I tell you what, Maša, from now on until the rest of your life – I am officially taking over setting the table – here, in front of witnesses.

DUNJA. That's a fantastic idea. We'll draw you a map of the kitchen.

VLADO. All right, all right, I get it. Though if you take into account the suppers Grandma Rose made plus holidays, it can't have been more than ten thousand. And that's a liberal estimate.

MAŠA *makes a face, about to lunge into a rant.*

LUCIJA. Mum, please, I'm starving.

VLADO. Hang on. We must do this properly.

VLADO *raises his glass and does a small 'announcement cough'.*

Before he can speak, noise from upstairs interrupts him. Loud sounds of heavy furniture being moved around. They look up with a sense of unease. The noise subsides, VLADO raises his glass again, LUCIJA gets ready to be toasted.

So. A toast to my daughters. Alisa who doesn't grace us with her presence often, which I suppose is how it must be. Regardless of how painful it is for us –

MAŠA. Vlado, really…

VLADO. A strange cycle befalls us. I remember back in the eighties when Dunja was working in Germany how excited we were to welcome her home once every year. Of course in Dunja's case she had a fifteen-hour drive from Düsseldorf and nowadays from London it's less than two hours, *and* on a low-cost airline, and yet –

ALISA. Shouldn't you be toasting Lucy?

VLADO. Yes, I'm getting to that, thank you. Tomorrow, Lucy, for you one life ends and another life begins. I can only hope that in Damjan you have made a wise choice and that you will have a happy life.

ALISA. Hear, hear!

VLADO. Hang on, I'm not finished yet. (*Pauses for effect.*) You have both chosen your paths. Mum and I take pride in never having tried to put pressure on you. Though she was always a bigger fan of the Summerhill book than I was but there you have it –

MAŠA. Vlado…

Glasses go up in the air.

VLADO. And now, all that's left for me to say is a word or two on the subject of marriage.

Glasses go back on the table.

What is marriage? It is a union with another human being with whom one can share the burden of life but equally, the joy and happiness of the said life. That's not to say that not being married is not a perfectly valid choice –

His body addresses ALISA.

And whoever thinks that marriage is easy is very much mistaken. It is a course in life, which demands great sacrifices –

MAŠA. What sacrifices?

VLADO. I'm sorry?

MAŠA. What exactly have you sacrificed?

VLADO. I mean, marriage as such.

MAŠA. I'd pay good money to hear what he's had to sacrifice.

VLADO. And even then it can go terribly wrong turning partners into enemies.

His body now addresses DUNJA.

DUNJA. That's if you marry a cunt.

MAŠA. Dunja, please, we agreed you wouldn't use that word.

DUNJA *lights a cigarette.* MAŠA *immediately starts waving the smoke away.*

VLADO. All a man needs is a true companion by his side who believes in him and supports him and there isn't an ordeal in this world he could not survive.

ALISA. What about women, Dad?

VLADO. I'm sorry?

ALISA. What about women?

VLADO. What about women?

ALISA. What does a woman need?

VLADO. I say 'man' I also mean 'woman'.

ALISA. Oh, I see.

LUCIJA. Dad, I had one soft-boiled egg today. Have mercy!

VLADO. So, in conclusion. Seek your happiness on your own terms, that's the best advice I can impart. But never forget to be there for each other. May you live long and prosper, my dear Lucija.

EVERYONE. Cheers!

VLADO. Or should I say, amen!

LUCIJA *snorts her irritation. But the glasses are brought together in a round of 'cheers'.* MAŠA *snaps a picture with her camera.*

*

Supper is almost over. MAŠA *takes the dishes through to the kitchen.* LUCIJA *helps out.* ALISA's *laptop sits opened on the table.* DUNJA *is looking at photographs on it.*

ALISA. Do people still do that? And when I say people, I mean men. Do they really still have stag nights?

LUCIJA *comes back in.*

LUCIJA. What do you mean?

ALISA. Well... the concept of the last night of freedom... marriage being a prison a man sort of capitulates in to... isn't it...

LUCIJA. Isn't it what?

ALISA. Stupid. A little offensive. Dated, at least.

VLADO. Not dated at all...

ALISA. Men are stags and women are hens?

LUCIJA. You didn't come to my hen night because you find the concept offensive?

ALISA. No. I had to work.

DUNJA. Things are different in the West.

LUCIJA. As she has pointed out many times. In case we missed it the three thousand times you pointed it out.

DUNJA *brushes it off with a puff of her cigarette.*

VLADO (*to* ALISA). Now, sweetheart, what's the word on us joining the EU up there?

ALISA. In Britain? Well, Dad, they're not holding their breath. That's if they're aware of us at all. We don't feature on their radar much... when it's not to do with beaches... or war criminals.

VLADO. That's a damn bloody injustice. A damn, damn bloody injustice. We have always been European, since the bloody Ottoman times. Yugoslavia was a respected European country –

MAŠA *enters with plates.*

DUNJA. Well, sort of respected.

VLADO. It was respected. The only Union we had a shot with. But no, that's when the pride comes out. 'They're screwing us over in Yugoslavia.' Hundreds of years we're screwed by whoever is big enough to screw us. We fight for independence and end up screwed worst by our own. And now we have to humiliate ourselves to be let into a Union from which any sane country with a survival instinct would want to get the hell away. It's a bloody travesty!

MAŠA. You know the Austrians bought the gas, the Hungarians bought the banks –

DUNJA. It's the other way around –

MAŠA. Regardless, we might as well have stayed in the Monarchy.

MAŠA *waves away the smoke as she exits to the kitchen.*

LUCIJA. I received a funny tweet from Slovenia saying 'Welcome Croats. We've fucked Yugoslavia, we'll do the same to Europe.'

She giggles.

ALISA (*to* VLADO). You always thought unions were a more progressive idea than nation states.

VLADO. I did and I do. Only in this case it's only a lesser of two evils.

ALISA. There are plenty of benefits to being in the EU.

LUCIJA. Quite a lot of people think it's the greater evil. Quite a lot of people don't want to blindly follow into another union.

VLADO. You say 'a lot'. You can't be sure those people on that thing are real.

DUNJA. Oh, Vlado...

LUCIJA. People on Facebook are real.

VLADO. If they are real and if an issue is worth protesting over, then go out into the street and protest. What is this anonymous, lazy, one-click stand everyone seems to be taking these days – take to the streets if –

LUCIJA. You want me to take to the streets?

VLADO. Yes. Well, no. I'm talking about the principle of the matter – she went out and sat on that square in front of the church, what was it –

ALISA. St Paul's –

LUCIJA. For all of four hours.

VLADO. It was very cold that day.

LUCIJA. Oh, what do you know?

VLADO. I looked it up on AccuWeather. It's very accurate.

ALISA. I went several times, but that's hardly relevant now. Dad, why would you encourage her to go out protesting against the EU?

VLADO. I wouldn't dream of it!

MAŠA *comes in with the cake.*

MAŠA. Have some cake, Vlado, and don't get too excited.

VLADO. It's the fate of a small nation. Always someone's… lapdog. To use a polite word. We should have fought for a confederacy. Imagine, just imagine if a confederate Yugoslavia had joined the European Union – just imagine the force.

DUNJA. Americans would never have allowed that. When the Soviet Bloc came down, Yugoslavia had to go!

MAŠA. I am vetoing this conversation.

VLADO. There's a curse on us and that's that.

MAŠA. Vlado!

VLADO. Cake. Yum.

DUNJA (*re: pictures on the laptop*). The flat looks lovely. Smallish, but lovely. Good neighbourhood then?

ALISA. Yes. Not fancy or anything. But vibrant.

DUNJA. Close to the centre?

ALISA. Yes. Fairly close.

LUCIJA. By helicopter.

ALISA. It's close to work and that's most important.

> DUNJA *slides the laptop over to* LUCIJA. *Half-sulking, she starts to look at pictures.*

> And work is good.

VLADO. Excellent. That's the most important thing. Cos we were getting a little worried –

MAŠA. Vlado...

VLADO. We were, because you don't want to overeducate yourself –

ALISA. School is the most important thing in the world. Is what you used to say every single day. That was your Headmaster Mantra.

VLADO. But with the purpose of propelling your life forward. And here you are, as grey-haired as a koala bear and you're still at school.

MAŠA. A PhD takes time, Vlado.

VLADO. I know how long a PhD takes. I have one, unless you've forgotten.

DUNJA. Who could forget that?

MAŠA. Yours took two years because you wouldn't have known what to do with yourself when they sacked you from the school.

VLADO. Unjustly.

MAŠA. And a PhD in England is not the same as PhD in Zagreb.

LUCIJA. Is it because things are different in the West?

VLADO. Didn't you say you were proud of me for not changing my convictions when it was fashionable to change them in '91?

MAŠA. I did, what's that got to do with anything?

VLADO (*under his breath*). It's the way you say 'sacked' –

LUCIJA (*to* ALISA). What's with the greys, seriously?

ALISA. I've dyed my hair since I was nineteen. I'm exhausted.

VLADO. Leave her alone. She has her reasons. We don't need to get into that.

ALISA. Exactly. I mean… what? What do you mean?

Noise is heard from upstairs. They look up with unease.

LUCIJA. She's doing it on purpose. I bet you she'll be at it all night, because she knows I need to get a good night's sleep for tomorrow.

ALISA. Who? Marko's mum?

LUCIJA. Yes. She's just being spiteful… I'm going to give her a call.

MAŠA. Lucija, let it go.

LUCIJA *is out the door.*

ALISA. Since when is Anita spiteful?

MAŠA. It's only they decided to move out on the very day of the wedding. Damjan asked her to wait but she insists it has to be tomorrow.

ALISA. Right. (*Pointing to the floor below.*) What about…?

MAŠA. We thought the Horaks would make a fuss, you know what they're like, but they actually left quite swiftly.

ALISA. They didn't make a fuss? Did someone have a gun to their head?

VLADO *gets up on his feet to toast.*

VLADO. May we gather together like this for years to come. And may we live to see another generation in this house. If only Grandma Rose and Granddad Aleksandar were with us.

MAŠA. And Karolina.

VLADO. And Karolina.

ALISA. And Boni.

VLADO. And sweet Boni, how we miss the sound of her little paws.

EVERYONE. Cheers.

LUCIJA *re-enters*.

LUCIJA. She says she wasn't aware of the noise. (*Raising her glass*.) Cheers.

MAŠA *starts cutting the cake*. ALISA *raises her glass and gets up*.

VLADO (*alarmed*). What are you doing?

ALISA. I want to say a few words.

VLADO. About what?

ALISA. If you let me say them, you'll see.

VLADO. As long as it's not an announcement.

MAŠA. Vlado, really…

VLADO. No, not 'Vlado really'. Every time she has an announcement, I end up with heart palpitations. There it is – a déjà vu. I'm getting heartburn just looking at you.

DUNJA. Vlado, you do get very dramatic –

VLADO. Do I? Was she not standing here like this when she announced that she was moving away to the end of the world? Then she was going to stay another year for an MA, then another three for a PhD. Then she simply informed us she'd got married, which was quite a shock –

ALISA. Unnecessarily –

VLADO. Well, I'm sorry. In my world it's not something you just do with just anyone, even if it was purely for administrative purposes –

ALISA. Dad, we have been over this a million –

VLADO. Not to mention you neglected to say that he was as dark as a moonless night.

ALISA *throws her arms in the air in exasperation.*

Well, excuse me for wanting to be informed about my son-in-law's background. About his heritage and and –

ALISA. He was not your son-in-law! He was just a man I married –

VLADO. Just like your mother, she used to fool around with those students from the non-aligned countries. Where was that guy from, Ethiopia?

MAŠA. Is there something wrong with that?

VLADO. Nothing wrong! But it deserves a mention. If she's going to go and live in Ethiopia.

ALISA. He was Jamaican! And I was never going to live in... Mum!

MAŠA. Vlado, here's a thought – let's let Alisa breathe and let's focus on the day that's ahead of us.

LUCIJA. Thank you.

VLADO. You think I'm old-fashioned and...

ALISA. Backward.

VLADO. Yes, that too, you've said that on a number of occasions.

ALISA. Only when you had it coming.

VLADO. You know, you could not have hoped for a more open-minded father. You put an old man through more than his fair share of controversies and he takes it all on the chin – who was the person who brought the discussion of your lesbianism to the table?

ALISA. I knew you'd be back on that! Because I stopped dying my hair?! I'm sorry, yes, I'm also over thirty and single.

VLADO. Personally, I thought that was very perceptive of me –

ALISA *sighs in frustration.*

If we examine the implications... So, yes, past thirty. And single. Save for that poor bastard upstairs who never recovered from the break-up with you, and the, as you said, non-romantic involvement with the… gentleman you called husband for a while.

ALISA. Marko, upstairs, never recovered from the front line, not me!

VLADO. He doesn't deserve to be judged, having been to hell and back –

DUNJA. At least he came back alive. Unlike poor Igor.

MAŠA. Poor poor Igor –

ALISA. Who's judging him? Nobody's judging him. Mum!

MAŠA. Vlado, arrive at a point, please.

ALISA. He put a knife to my throat! I know, he went through a war on the front lines, he was messed up when he came back, he didn't mean to harm me, but what was I supposed to do?

VLADO. He suffered a trauma and proceeded to inflict a trauma on you. And traumatic events in one's intimate relationships have been known to play a part in sexual orientation –

ALISA. Does anyone monitor his use of the internet?

VLADO. On the other hand, there have always been these ladies you lived with.

ALISA. Flatmates. Women I chose to live with over men because men are pigs. When you live with men, you live with a whole universe of microorganisms.

VLADO. That to me sounds like a lesbian argument. Anyway, attractive young women, single, lonely, in a foreign land…

ALISA. You do understand what you're describing is a plot line of a porn film –

VLADO. Now that's uncalled for.

LUCIJA. You fool around a couple of times, doesn't mean anything –

ALISA *looks at* LUCIJA *in disbelief.*

ALISA. What I actually think is that gender doesn't matter, but that is obviously a conversation for a different meridian.

LUCIJA. 'A different meridian.'

ALISA. Shut up, if you had kept your mouth shut, I would never have burdened him with that particular interval of my life.

LUCIJA. He was about to pull out my fingernails. I buckled.

ALISA. Please! You started ratting on me before you could handle solid food.

MAŠA. All right, that's enough of that.

VLADO. I will never understand why dinner conversation with you lot always turns so damn contentious. Why can't we have some pleasant anecdotes for example, some pleasant, non-confrontational –

ALISA. You started it.

VLADO. All I wanted was to toast to my daughter on the day before her wedding and keep things light and simple.

ALISA. Light and simple?!

VLADO. All I ever hope for, actually, is a kindred male spirit in this house. Why that's such a definite impossibility, I shall never understand. Poor Marko might have turned into a great chap if the war hadn't screwed with his head; you didn't even think to introduce your temporary… colleague…

ALISA. Dad –

VLADO. You think it's easy? You think it has been easy for me?

ALISA. A whole battalion of women looking after your needs. I feel for you.

VLADO. Four generations and not a single male offspring in this family! If that were the average, the species would disappear. I'm sure statistically, we're due a lesbian. As a sort of a… an… evolutionary turnaround –

MAŠA *checks her watch.*

MAŠA. Vlado –

DUNJA. I don't get how that could help the species –

VLADO. No, well, no. But I gather that's not a popular thing to say these days.

LUCIJA and ALISA give up and start giggling.

MAŠA. Vlado, the Stalin documentary is on. Weren't you going to tape it?

VLADO checks his watch.

VLADO. Damn it! What are you two laughing about? Easy to laugh at old Dad, isn't it?

Now MAŠA and DUNJA join in the laughter. VLADO gets up.

Oh, yes, laugh away. As long as I amuse you. A person tries to understand your bizarre ways and all he gets is ridicule. Your mother was the same. And Karolina. Even Boni had no respect for me, the little barking whore.

The laughter intensifies. VLADO exits, demonstratively. The laughter subsides. A therapeutic sense of relief.

ALISA. Well. Let's see how he likes living with the good dose of testosterone that is his future son-in-law!

She giggles, the others don't find it as funny as she intended.

VLADO re-enters.

VLADO (*to* LUCIJA). The new telly doesn't work. The VCR is not responding.

LUCIJA. Dad, I showed you yesterday. It's a new system. It's digital.

VLADO. I did everything you said. It doesn't work! And now I'm going to miss my Stalin documentary.

ALISA. Dad, leave Stalin alone for a moment, come and sit down –

VLADO. I will not leave Stalin alone. These tapes are for you ungrateful… For posterity. I have every single important piece of our history on tape. I have the declaration of

Croatia's independence, I have the fall of Vukovar, I have Srebrenica, I have Tuđman's death, I have NATO in Serbia, I have Kosovo. I don't have the 14th congress of the Central Committee in 1990, but who'd have thought.

DUNJA. No one could have known.

VLADO. And that whole day… Best forgotten.

He waves his hand as if brushing off a bad memory.

If Tito hadn't said no to Stalin in 1948, who knows what would have happened with this family. Dunja may not have even been born.

LUCIJA. Come on, let's have a look.

LUCIJA *and* VLADO *exit.*

ALISA. Dunja wouldn't have been born?

MAŠA. Ah, it's an old story. Your Grandma Rose had an admirer among Tito's generals. Before Dunja was born.

DUNJA. More than an admirer.

MAŠA. No, we don't know that. All we know is that they were comrades in the resistance. Whilst Granddad was…

DUNJA. Effectively on the other side.

MAŠA. The General was around for a while after the war –

DUNJA. Threatening to whisk her away. Your granddad used to be so jealous of him.

MAŠA. Then the General made a wrong call in 1948. Didn't think Tito was going to break off from Stalin –

DUNJA. Didn't change his tune in time –

MAŠA. Ended up in prison.

DUNJA. Poor guy.

MAŠA. Poor poor guy.

DUNJA. Karl used to tease me I literally owed my life to Tito.

The sisters giggle.

ALISA. I saw Uncle Karl, I mean Karl, in the paper on the plane over.

DUNJA. Yes. Karl in the Ministry of European and Foreign Affairs. It's like a Monty Python sketch. We were almost going to have him at the wedding.

ALISA. I'm sorry?

DUNJA. They seem to be networking events, weddings. Damjan thought it would be good for business. Lucy managed to convince him it was a bad idea.

ALISA. Right.

MAŠA. I'll get coffee. (*Exiting.*) You should try on the veil. Just in case.

DUNJA *throws her a damning look*. MAŠA *exits*.

ALISA. The veil?

DUNJA (*hesitantly*). Yes… I'm going to be the… False Bride.

ALISA. The what?

DUNJA. The False Bride. You know. When the groom arrives tomorrow, with the entourage and the string band… To 'buy the bride'. The old custom.

ALISA. Right. The old custom.

DUNJA. It's for Lucy and Damjan. It's just for fun.

ALISA. What is it about him that makes people lose their spine?

DUNJA. I'm sorry?

ALISA. Nothing. Sorry. (*Pause.*) It'll be fun to have the whole house to ourselves, I guess. Now that Damjan has bought it. And the neighbours are moving out. Our little family sprawling all around it like some feudal barons. Fraternity and unity, that's a fun old custom, too, isn't it?

DUNJA. People buy houses nowadays. Times are changing.

ALISA. Times are always changing.

DUNJA. Yes. And I suppose if you found yourself back in 1945 when we were allocated two rooms and all three families in the house shat in the same toilet you would have objections to that too.

ALISA *stops, momentarily lost for words.* MAŠA *re-enters with coffee on a tray.*

God, for once your mother is going to have a little space to herself.

MAŠA. What's that?

DUNJA. Nothing.

VLADO *and* LUCIJA *enter,* VLADO *somewhat remorseful in appearance.*

LUCIJA. Problem solved.

MAŠA. It's working?

LUCIJA. Of course it's working. It's the best thing on the market.

VLADO. Maša, did you want me to tape something for you?

MAŠA. My show on Discovery at eleven.

VLADO. Of course. Consider it done.

VLADO *hovers.*

If anyone else has anything they'd like me to tape…

DUNJA. No, Vlado. I'll come and watch your Stalin programme in a minute.

VLADO. Lovely. You're all welcome to join us. It's a cracking piece, this one. Or if anything else needs taping, I'm… er… available.

ALISA. Okay, Dad. Thanks. That's very kind of you.

VLADO *exits. Noise is heard from upstairs.* LUCIJA *throws her arms up in exasperation.*

I'm surprised they agreed to move.

LUCIJA. They should count themselves lucky. Upstairs is falling apart. It will take a fortune to renovate.

DUNJA. I'll go take a peek at Stalin.

She exits. MAŠA *drinks her coffee.* LUCIJA *gets a text on her mobile. She giggles.*

LUCIJA. It's from Damjan. I have to call him.

She hops away. Silence.

MAŠA. Come have some more cake. You don't have to get into a wedding dress tomorrow.

ALISA *acquiesces.* MAŠA *smiles and gets on with cutting the cake with great pleasure.*

Scene Three

November, 1945.

Evening.

The living room in the house is cold and dusty. ROSE, *aged twenty-seven, wearing simple, plain, forties clothes, stands in the middle of the room – a firm stance, as if reclaiming the space. She holds a baby in her arms. Some luggage sits in the middle of the room. Holding the baby, she starts taking sheets off the furniture to reveal once-fancy period pieces. She stops by the clock. The time has stopped. She feels the case, moves the handle, nothing happens.*

ALEKSANDAR *enters, thirty years old, his body language ill-at-ease in this place. He walks with a slight limp. He brings in a simple, wooden cradle and puts in on the floor.*

ROSE. You've been gone long.

ALEKSANDAR. It got dark, the fog came down. I'll leave a trail of crumbs next time.

ROSE. It's up the hill and straight ahead from the main square. It's easy.

ALEKSANDAR. It's easy for you townfolk.

ROSE *takes a blanket from a bundle and places it in the crib. She puts the baby in.*

ROSE. Where's Mother?

ALEKSANDAR. Outside, sitting on the trunk.

ROSE *shakes her head.* ALEKSANDAR *sits at the table. Tense. He lights a cigarette.*

All this space for just two people.

ROSE *opens a cupboard, she looks at some dishes, some are broken. She picks up a small bowl and places it in front of* ALEKSANDAR.

ROSE. Until we find an ashtray.

ALEKSANDAR *looks at it – is it or isn't it an ashtray – and taps the ashes into it.*

The house belonged to a Theodor Amruš. He was a solicitor in the Austro-Hungarian Monarchy and later in the Kingdom of the Serbs, Croats and the Slovenes. Then he was part of Parliament and the Croatian Peasant Party, then, from what I heard, he lined up with Pavelić and the Nazis and fled recently.

ALEKSANDAR. Busy bee.

ROSE. Very.

ALEKSANDAR. And the family?

ROSE. The wife died in second childbirth. The lady of the house was his daughter. Karolina. She employed Mother. There was a son who studied somewhere abroad. England I think. I don't know what became of them. Where *is* Mother?

ROSE *looks out of the window. She sighs and then walks out of the room with a purpose.*

ALEKSANDAR *goes to the cupboard and inspects a plate, a bowl, a broken glass. He unpacks a bundle of photographs. One is framed.* ROSE *and* ALEKSANDAR *on their wedding day, 1940. He puts it on display.*

ROSE *comes back in,* MONIKA, *forty-five, reluctantly follows.*

Come on, Mother, come in.

MONIKA *enters. She walks around, takes a sheet off a sofa, she looks at it all as if it were a ghost house.*

MONIKA (*to* ALEKSANDAR). That's not an ashtray.

ALEKSANDAR. There is no ashtray.

MONIKA *walks over to the cupboard, opens a drawer and rummages about. She produces an ashtray. She puts it on the table. She starts collecting broken pieces.*

ROSE. Mother, let go of that now, please.

MONIKA. What did you bring us here for?

ROSE. To live.

MONIKA (*shaking her head*). To live. In the house for the gentry.

ROSE. There is no more gentry.

MONIKA. They just let you have it?

ROSE. The Party let me choose a place to live.

MONIKA. Just like that?

ROSE. I've earned it.

ALEKSANDAR. How?

ROSE. I'm sorry?

ALEKSANDAR. I said, how?

ROSE. I was sent to Comrade Marinko's office. It's at the National Theatre. I don't know why. He is the head of housing. (*Pause.*) It's how it's done. The Party looks after us all. Makes sure we get a roof over our heads.

ALEKSANDAR. And they let everyone choose, just like that.

ROSE *has the key to the house in her hand.*

ROSE. There was a mountain of house keys in the office. On a table. Hundreds, thousands. Comrade Marinko said, pick one. Then I saw the address on this one. And I remembered. I was born here. Isn't that right?

MONIKA. Yes. That's right.

ROSE (*to* ALEKSANDAR). They turned her out when I was only two days old.

ALEKSANDAR. Why? What did you do?

MONIKA. Ah, I don't remember. It was a long time ago.

ROSE. She didn't do anything. She was a servant. They threw her out because they could.

ALEKSANDAR *lights another cigarette.* ROSE *takes her shoes off and sits down with a pained look on her face.*

MONIKA. It wasn't like that. What's wrong?

ROSE. It's nothing. What was it like then?

MONIKA. Water under the bridge. Leave it alone. Are your feet sore?

MONIKA *approaches* ROSE *with a glass bottle and some cloth. She kneels next to* ROSE, *she pulls her socks off. Reluctantly* ROSE *lets* MONIKA *tend to her feet.*

ROSE. You're right. We haven't come here to look into the past. This room and the one next, that belongs to us now. The kitchen and the bathroom we share with whoever else arrives. One day perhaps we'll build our own.

ALEKSANDAR. What about the garden? Whose is the garden?

ROSE. Everyone's.

ALEKSANDAR. It's big. Big enough to put a coop in.

MONIKA. A coop. In the middle of a town.

ALEKSANDAR. So what if it's the middle of a town? I won't be embarrassed about reasonable things.

MONIKA (*to* ROSE). Camphor oil will draw the pain out.

ALEKSANDAR. Just because that's not how they used to do things in this house. In their bourgeois times. If it makes sense to have a coop, we'll have a coop.

ROSE. Who's going to look after chickens and hens –

ALEKSANDAR. And turkeys. We could fit in a couple of turkeys –

ROSE. We're at work all day, Mother looks after the baby, she
goes to work the moment I get home… I don't think we'll
have a coop. Mother, that's enough. It's all right, it's good.
Get off your knees.

She says it a little harsher than she intended. MONIKA
retreats.

(*Softer.*) Can you check on the baby?

MONIKA *looks in on the baby.*

MONIKA. She's asleep. Like a little angel. (*Pause.*) She should
have a name.

ROSE. She will.

ALEKSANDAR *takes a sheet off a painting. It's the portrait
of* KAROLINA. MONIKA *almost gasps at the sight of it.*

What's the matter?

MONIKA. This is Miss Karolina. She was the lady of the
house. That was her favourite dress.

ROSE. She reminds me of someone.

ALEKSANDAR. They all looked the same. In those clothes,
with that hair. Like circus freaks.

ROSE. We'll take it down.

MONIKA. It belongs on this wall.

ROSE. It used to belong on this wall. I don't want her watching
over me all the time. They had creepy taste, those people.
Look at her, she can barely breathe under the weight of… I
don't know what.

MONIKA. Do you know where they are? Mr Amruš and the
rest of them?

ROSE. Not for certain. A number of collaborators fled to
Argentina.

MONIKA. Why there?

ROSE. I don't know, Mother. That's where they go. Croatian
émigrés. He probably had relatives or something.

ALEKSANDAR. I have some relatives in Argentina. Buenos
    Aires. Only distant. You know what it means, 'buenos aires'?
    Fair winds.

ROSE. Are you thinking of emigrating?

ALEKSANDAR. No! No. I only meant, I wonder what it's like
    – starting a new life. In a new country.

ROSE. We are starting a new life in a new country. But unlike
    them, we don't have to run halfway across the world to do it.
    And I'd keep quiet about your Argentinean lot. Who knows
    what kind of company they keep there.

    Crestfallen, ALEKSANDAR *goes through the luggage.*

ALEKSANDAR. Where did you put the wine?

ROSE. In the kitchen.

    ALEKSANDAR *waits.*

    One floor below.

MONIKA. I'll get it.

ALEKSANDAR. No. I want to have a look around.

    He exits. MONIKA *opens a drawer and picks up a key. She
    goes to the clock, inserts the key and starts winding it.*

MONIKA. What is the time?

    ROSE *checks her wristwatch.*

ROSE. Twenty past eight.

    MONIKA *sets the clock. It starts ticking.*

MONIKA. Mr Amruš was very much in favour of the Serbs and
    Croats uniting when the first war ended.

ROSE. That was a quarter of a century ago.

MONIKA. Ms Karolina could not have been a collaborator. She
    was very smart.

ROSE. I'm sure they thought it was a smart choice.

MONIKA. No. I don't believe it. She was kind and clever.

ROSE. And yet she turned you out with a two-day-old baby.

MONIKA *bends down to check on* ROSE*'s feet.*

MONIKA. Keep still. It needs to work itself in.

ROSE. It's fine. I feel better.

MONIKA *looks up at* ROSE.

MONIKA. Love, it's not right the way you speak to him.

ROSE *is quiet.*

What if he leaves you? You have a baby. Who will have you?

ROSE. Mother… (*Pause.*) Please, get off the floor. I can't bear to look at you, on your knees every five minutes!

MONIKA *gets up, hurt.* ALEKSANDAR *walks in with a demijohn in a wicker cover and some glasses.* MONIKA *immediately jumps to his assistance. She pours the wine.*

ALEKSANDAR. This Amruš fellow, how long since he fled?

ROSE. I don't know. Before the end of the war I expect.

ALEKSANDAR. The ashes in the stove are fresh. Yesterday's by the looks of it.

ROSE. Right. Well… perhaps it's…

MONIKA (*alarmed*)….What?

ROSE (*overcome by nerves*). Well, how should I know? Perhaps there's someone else already moving in. Another family like us. I don't know.

MONIKA. All right, all right. Don't raise your voice. You'll wake up the baby.

ALEKSANDAR *raises his glass.*

ALEKSANDAR. To our health.

He drinks. ROSE *pours some wine for herself.*

ROSE. Mother, will you have some?

MONIKA. I'll start bringing in our things.

ROSE. Just put them inside. We'll bring them up together.

MONIKA *exits*. ALEKSANDAR *and* ROSE *remain at the table in silence. Sipping the wine.*

ALEKSANDAR. We can't keep calling her baby.

ROSE. It suits her.

ALEKSANDAR. It suits her now. We don't know what she'll be like when she's older. (*Pointedly.*) Whom she'll take after.

ROSE (*ignoring*). She does have an appetite.

ROSE *looks at the baby in the crib.*

ALEKSANDAR. The name is important. See how it made my life hell. My mother and her royalist delusions. Aleksandar King.

ROSE. She couldn't have known. The Prince Regent was young and promising, I'm sure she meant well.

ALEKSANDAR (*tentatively*). Perhaps we should think of a neutral name. A name that would suit her in any given set of circumstances.

ROSE. It's best you don't talk like that.

ALEKSANDAR. I'm just saying. From experience.

ROSE. I know what you're saying. What I'm saying is it makes you sound like you lack conviction. Which, in your case, is particularly dangerous. (*Regarding his photographs.*) And put those away, you'll get us all killed.

ALEKSANDAR *slams his fist on the table, consumed with helpless anger.*

ALEKSANDAR. Do you have any idea what it's like for me?

ROSE*'s body immediately tenses up. The intimacy between them is tenuous.*

ROSE. Be quiet, you'll wake her up!

ALEKSANDAR. She never cries, anyway.

*Silence. ROSE inspects her feet in the cloths. This
debilitating situation annoys her. ALEKSANDAR pours
them more wine. Silent, he watches ROSE. He takes her
hand and strokes it, awkwardly. He reaches for her neck. His
hand creeps down towards her breast. He tries to slide it
inside her blouse. Tense, she glances at the door and
manoeuvres her body out of his grip. Immediately he pulls
back, offended.*

ROSE. Mother will be back any moment.

ALEKSANDAR *drinks his wine.* ROSE *is silent.*

ALEKSANDAR. I don't know why you bother with me.

I'll drag you down all your life.

ROSE. Nonsense. Sasha, please.

ALEKSANDAR. The shrapnel in the leg. I'll never even walk
properly again.

ROSE. Who cares about that? You're alive.

ALEKSANDAR. The job in the factory – it was you.

ROSE. You are the best tailor I've ever met.

ALEKSANDAR. How many have you met?

ROSE. They needed a good tailor. They wanted to hire you.

ALEKSANDAR. I should have been the one to sort out where
we live.

ROSE. What difference does it make? We got the flat.

ALEKSANDAR. I should have gone to the woods, too, that's
what you're thinking.

ROSE. I'm not thinking anything. We both did what we could
manage.

ALEKSANDAR. You managed.

ROSE. You were gone. I was alone. I couldn't just sit and hope
I don't get killed.

ALEKSANDAR. I was drafted.

ROSE. I know.

ALEKSANDAR. If you desert, you get court-martialled. You get executed. I was drafted.

ROSE. I know.

ALEKSANDAR. I was a Communist in my heart long before you ever knew what it was and I'm now a… a…

ROSE. Sasha… I have never accused you of anything.

ALEKSANDAR. But it's there. It will always be there. Hanging above my head.

His shaky hands firmly grip a photograph.

That uniform.

ALEKSANDAR *drinks more.*

If we had gone back to the country, to my family –

ROSE. I will not have my child shovelling shit all her life!

ALEKSANDAR. Plenty of shit in the city.

He focuses on his glass.

I won't have *him* take care of us. It's not right.

ROSE. Really, Sasha, stop talking and don't be ungrateful.

ALEKSANDAR. It's not right.

ROSE. The General is a good man. He wants to see merits rewarded. That's all.

ALEKSANDAR. Is she mine?

ROSE. Sasha –

ALEKSANDAR. Tell me the truth.

ROSE. I told you the truth.

ALEKSANDAR. That's all I ask. Tell me the truth so I know. If she's mine. Or his. I need to know.

ROSE. Sasha –

ALEKSANDAR. I need to know. The truth. Whatever it is. But I need to know.

ROSE. I was pregnant when I went to the woods. She is our
child.

ALEKSANDAR *slams his fist again. The baby is heard from
the crib.* ROSE *wants to get up but the cloths around her feet
prevent her. He grabs her hands.*

ALEKSANDAR. Just tell me, Rose. Just tell me the truth. It's
all right. Whatever it is. But I need to know it. That's all I'm
asking. Nothing more. Just the truth.

ROSE *gets up with determination. She rips the cloths off her
feet and frowns in pain. A bucket sits next to the fireplace.
She grabs it and throws the cloths inside.*

ROSE. There was a night when she was only about a month old,
we were hiding in some ditch, south of Karlovac. The
Germans were not more than twenty feet away. I had her in
my arms. And I see her waking up. If she cries, we're all
dead. Everyone sees it. They stare at her and I know
someone will pull a knife and slit her throat before she gives
us away. So I pull out my breast, I stick it in her mouth and
she begins to suck. Like an angel, oblivious to the fact she
was seconds away from death.

ALEKSANDAR. Rose…

ROSE. Now, you listen to me, Aleksandar King. You had some
bad luck in life. You have that unfortunate name. You were
on the unfortunate side in war. You had a grim childhood.
You and me both. Never enough food, never enough warmth.
Never a kind word. These damned deformed feet since I was
six years old. A bastard. People always whispering. Like
Mother – keep your head down, out of the way. We had no
say in that life we'd been given. But now we have a say. No
woman will be turned out into the street with an infant to
fend for herself. My mother will never be a servant again.
Our daughter will never be a servant to anyone. She will
grow up in a free country, with all the rights in the world.
She will go to school, she will have a happy childhood and a
better life. We made it through the war. If we have to roll up
our sleeves now to make that happen I am ready. I am ready
with all my heart and soul. And I am proud. But I'm telling

you now, Sasha, once and for ever – I will not let you ruin our lives. If you torture me I swear on our daughter's life, I will leave you. I will take her and she and I will leave.

ALEKSANDAR *is silent, defeated.*

Adamantly, ROSE *brings the bucket closer. She takes a match from* ALEKSANDAR, *lights it and drops it in the bucket. Flames rise up.*

This subject is closed. We don't dwell on it any more. What happened to you there – (*Points at the photographs.*) ends now and is not to be mentioned again. We are not going to live our lives in shame.

She snaps the photographs from ALEKSANDAR's *hands and drops them in the bucket.*

They watch the photographs burn. The flames dwindle. ROSE *looks in on the baby in the crib.*

She's awake. And she doesn't cry. Poor little thing.

ROSE *rocks the crib gently.* ALEKSANDAR *gets up and joins her. Awkwardly she puts her hand on his shoulder.*

ALEKSANDAR. How about 'Maša'? You can't go wrong with a Russian name.

ROSE. Maša.

ALEKSANDAR. Maša.

Scene Four

January, 1990.

Evening, nine o'clock.

Bedroom.

MAŠA *sits in front of an open wardrobe. She is folding some clothes, taking in the smell. She is in her early forties.* DUNJA *comes in, also a woman in her early forties, a plate with strudel in her hand. Both women are dressed in black.* MAŠA *wears a skirt and a blouse tucked in. It's a simple and not very flattering outfit.* DUNJA*'s outfit, though demure, is certainly more in keeping with the fashion trends of 1990.*

DUNJA. There's no need to sort this out now. I mean, why do it now?

  MAŠA *is quiet.*

Have some strudel. It's delicious. Did you make it?

MAŠA. Yes.

DUNJA. And the pie?

MAŠA. Yes. And the cheesecake and the sandwiches. Who else? Vlado thinks storks fly in the food. Alisa has all but stopped speaking to everyone and Lucija, well, food is not exactly safe around her.

DUNJA. Why do you feed them so much?

MAŠA. I don't 'feed them so much'. They're hungry they eat.

DUNJA. They won't thank you for it one day.

  DUNJA *lights a cigarette. Immediately,* MAŠA *starts waving the smoke away, trying to do it inconspicuously. She goes back to sorting out things in the wardrobe.*

MAŠA. Our mum never indulged us…

DUNJA. Christ, Maša, there was nothing to indulge in. She was just frugal.

MAŠA. She could have been a little less frugal with tenderness.

DUNJA. Ah, what the hell did she know about tenderness?

Silence. More sorting out. DUNJA *picks at the strudel.*

MAŠA. How is Dad? Has he come out?

DUNJA. The sobbing got to him, he's exhausted. Did you see the telegram? From the General?

MAŠA *smiles.*

MAŠA. Yes. Best keep it from Dad.

DUNJA. I put it in my bag.

Silence.

You know, I hope it wasn't just… camaraderie. I hope Mum had a bit of variety in her life. Instead of just the one man… like serving a sentence.

MAŠA. If she hadn't been pregnant with me when they met perhaps she would have gone with the General.

DUNJA. So. Once again, you are my saviour. Not Tito.

DUNJA *chuckles.* MAŠA *smiles ruefully.*

Now listen here. I'll send you some good-quality hair dye from Germany. I don't want you using Henna any more. Women in Yugoslavia look like a big skulk of foxes. It's freakish. Like some sort of a tragic social experiment.

MAŠA *strokes the dresses in silence.*

MAŠA. You know the past ten years I think we could barely stand each other.

DUNJA. You and I?

MAŠA. No. Not you and I. Mum and I.

DUNJA. Living together gets like that.

MAŠA. Maybe it was just the lack of space. Before Karolina signed over her half and moved into a home, Christ, we were like sardines in a tin.

Pause.

Mum looked after the house and the girls while I was at work. I don't know what I would have done without her and now she's gone and it's too late to tell her that.

DUNJA. Maša. She knew.

MAŠA. I resented her because… because they loved you more. Because they taught me to look after you from the day you were born. And then you flew away, you made this great life for yourself in Germany and you never looked back.

DUNJA. I looked back!

MAŠA. No, I know… I know. It's how I felt. It's not you.

DUNJA. Maša, they didn't love me more.

MAŠA. Dad did. Perhaps Mum didn't but she didn't know how to show it.

DUNJA. The only difference was I never let people put me down and you were always trying to make everybody happy.

MAŠA. Is that a flaw?

DUNJA. It is if it harms you.

MAŠA. I guess that's your German outlook, isn't it?

Silence.

DUNJA *picks up her plate, suggesting she's about to leave.*

Dunja –

DUNJA. Yes?

MAŠA *struggles to articulate her thoughts.*

MAŠA. I don't know what's wrong with me. I don't think anybody has ever felt this lonely.

DUNJA *stops in her tracks, taken aback.*

Is that normal?

Speechless, DUNJA *struggles to find an answer.*

I feel like everything around me is… sort of… underwater.

DUNJA *stares at* MAŠA. MAŠA *looks at her, pleading not to be left hanging.*

LUCIJA *enters, interrupting, unaware. She is a girl of twelve, chubby and a little whiny.*

LUCIJA. Mum! Is it true that Grandma Rose was sent to work as a slave when she was five years old?

MAŠA. What? Where did you get that?

KAROLINA, *a lady of about ninety, wheels herself into the room in her wheelchair. Neatly dressed,* KAROLINA *wears a little too much fine jewellery and a small black hat on her head, her bright-red hair, still as red as in the portrait, arranged in a bun.*

Karolina!

KAROLINA. She ought to know the truth.

MAŠA *rolls her eyes and puts her arms around* LUCIJA. LUCIJA *has a Polaroid camera around her neck. She takes it off.*

LUCIJA. They were going to amputate her feet?

KAROLINA. It's important you listen and not exaggerate. The truth is often dramatic enough. It was her toes. She suffered severe frostbite and she very nearly had her *toes* amputated.

MAŠA. Karolina!

KAROLINA. They must know what it was like to be a girl. It's their history.

DUNJA. She'd have been sent away if she'd been a boy. (*To* LUCIJA.) Your great-grandma Monika was very poor. In this house where you now live, she worked as a maid. She couldn't afford to keep a child.

KAROLINA. Girls have always been considered a burden.

MAŠA. I have always wanted girls.

LUCIJA. I could do with a brother instead of Alisa.

KAROLINA. Brothers can be a sore disappointment.

LUCIJA *puts the camera on the table.*

LUCIJA. Mum, you know how Grandma Rose was a partisan, right?

MAŠA. Yes.

LUCIJA. Well, Boris Marić at school says that partisans were criminals.

MAŠA. Boris Marić is an idiot. And his parents are idiots. Don't say that at school.

LUCIJA. I already told him he was an idiot. Then he said I was a fucking Commie and my dad was a fucking Commie and that our time has passed.

MAŠA. I suppose his idiot father would make a better headmaster.

DUNJA. The little wanker.

LUCIJA. I said that too.

MAŠA. Dunja! Lucy, don't use language like that. And don't engage with him.

LUCIJA. Why not? I –

MAŠA. Because you don't stoop to that level.

LUCIJA (*sulky*). Alisa's going to have her feet amputated if she stays in the garden for much longer.

MAŠA. What's she doing out in the garden?

LUCIJA. What do you think? She's with Marko. And she's only wearing her leather jacket. Because she looks fat in her coat.

MAŠA *heads out*.

DUNJA. Maša?

MAŠA *stops, she looks back at* DUNJA. DUNJA *hesitates.* MAŠA *leaves.* LUCIJA *leaves the camera on the table and runs after* MAŠA. *The camera almost drops to the floor.* DUNJA *grabs it in time and places it securely on the table.*

LUCIJA (*off*). She's told Marko she is going to Vienna to see Depeche Mode in concert.

MAŠA (*off.*) The hell she is.

DUNJA. What are you doing? Why do you fill her head with this nonsense?

KAROLINA. She asked. About Rose. She said Grandma Rose had funny feet.

DUNJA. When I was afraid of penicillin shots, you told me, in detail, how they attached blood-sucking leeches to your body when you were young.

KAROLINA. I wanted you to appreciate modern medicine.

DUNJA. I had nightmares for years.

KAROLINA. Nonsense. You were tough. And so is Lucy. There is muscle under that fat. I want her to appreciate a carefree childhood. It's not to be taken for granted. I was about Alisa's age when my father almost had me married off to some poor Austrian sod only to strengthen the ties with the Monarchy. The Austro-Hungarian Monarchy, which collapsed two years later. Thank heavens my groom-to-be croaked before the match went through. Spanish flu I think. The only time I met him, he went to kiss my hand and spat blood on it.

DUNJA. It was tuberculosis.

KAROLINA. So you heard it before. You can hear it again. There was no choice. Now there is. (*Pause.*) What you put up with is a choice.

DUNJA. It's not that simple.

KAROLINA. It's simple enough. You don't want to get to ninety and look back and think, good heavens, I had a choice down the line.

DUNJA (*snaps*). Wasn't throwing Rose and Grandma Monika out on the street a choice you made? The famous toe-freeze would never happened...

　　KAROLINA *gasps*. DUNJA *stops, remorseful*. LUCIJA *barges back in*.

LUCIJA (*to* DUNJA). She's such a moron. How on earth Marko can like her...

　　LUCIJA *picks up her camera, then notices the strudel on the plate and starts on it.* KAROLINA *looks shattered*.

KAROLINA. I have spent most of my life making amends.

DUNJA. I know. I'm sorry. I didn't mean that.

DUNJA *hovers, awkwardly. She squeezes* KAROLINA*'s shoulder.*

What's going on out there?

LUCIJA (*mouth full of strudel*). Uncle Karl is talking. I don't exactly know what about.

DUNJA. Sounds about right.

LUCIJA. He says Auntie Lina is an aristocrat. And we should all be proud of that. Alisa is explaining something about Napoleon to him.

KAROLINA. One spends half a century ashamed of one's background, now one's meant to advertise it again. This world...

DUNJA. I should go keep an eye on his drinking. Come along, Lucy.

LUCIJA. When I finish this.

DUNJA *looks at her, disapproving, but lets it go.*

DUNJA. Hurry up then.

DUNJA *leaves.* KAROLINA *watches* LUCIJA *tenderly, as* LUCIJA *works on the strudel.*

KAROLINA. Are you happy, Lucija? Are you having a happy childhood?

LUCIJA *looks up, puzzled.*

LUCIJA. Yes. Not so much during the week but on the weekends, I guess so. I'm pretty happy when Alisa's away and I have the room to myself.

KAROLINA. Why not during the week?

LUCIJA. School.

KAROLINA. And you don't like that?

LUCIJA. Nobody likes going to school. Well, Alisa does. That tells you enough.

KAROLINA. When I was a girl, only boys went to school. Girls stayed at home. Learnt sewing and embroidery. How to sit properly. I wanted to learn history and politics. Philosophy maybe. So that I may have some independence, you see. But my papa sent my brother to Cambridge. We made a pact before he left. When he returns he will convince Papa to send me to college, too. Four years I waited. Embroidering napkins. But, by the time he came back, he'd forgotten about the pact. He had other interests.

KAROLINA *wanders off in her thoughts. Then she snaps out and takes* LUCIJA *by the hand.*

Lucy... listen to me. I don't know what's going to happen. The world is... unpredictable. But all of this should be yours. It should stay in the family. Remember that. Will you remember that?

LUCIJA. I will.

Scene Five

November, 1945.

Night-time.

Ten o'clock. The clock ticks in the dark, quiet house. MONIKA *sleeps on the divan.* ROSE *and* ALEKSANDAR *on a mattress. The baby in the crib. A figure moves across the room like a ghost. There is a creak on the floor.* MONIKA *bolts up in her bed.*

MONIKA (*whispers*). Rose. Rose.

ROSE. Yes?

MONIKA. Did you hear that?

ROSE. Hear what?

MONIKA *starts to lower herself back into bed. Another creak is heard.*

ALEKSANDAR. I heard that.

MONIKA. I'm telling you.

ROSE. It's probably just floorboards.

MONIKA. Floorboards squeak when they're being trod on.

As ALEKSANDAR *gets out of bed, the figure brushes past him and now everyone can sense it. Instinctively* ALEKSANDAR *grabs the figure. There is some commotion and panicked breathing.* ROSE *turns the light on. It's* KAROLINA *(forty-seven) in a long nightgown, long, messy red hair, eerie like an apparition.* ROSE *immediately goes to the crib.*

Miss Karolina?

ALEKSANDAR *releases her with a gasp.* KAROLINA *stares for a moment, and then runs away.*

Dear Lord, we've woken up the ghosts.

ROSE (*getting up, putting a coat on*). That's no ghost.

She and ALEKSANDAR *leave the room after* KAROLINA. MONIKA *lingers, shaken, then follows.*

Scene Six

November, 1945.

Same evening, a little later.

In a small bedroom. KAROLINA, MONIKA, ROSE *and* ALEKSANDAR. KAROLINA *stands next to the bed.* ALEKSANDAR *sits on a chair in the corner.* ROSE *looks out the window, thinking.* MONIKA *hovers. They've been here a while, debating.* KAROLINA *shivers.*

MONIKA. It's freezing in here. I'll go light the fire.

ROSE. Mother.

MONIKA. Yes?

ROSE. It's not your job.

MONIKA. Do I leave her to freeze?

ROSE. I'm sure she knows how to light a fire.

KAROLINA. True. I've learnt.

MONIKA. Ah, nonsense.

ALEKSANDAR. Mother, leave the fire just now.

> MONIKA *complies.* ROSE *sits down on a chair, her feet sore.* KAROLINA *perches on her bed.*

ROSE. So. How long have you been here?

> KAROLINA *won't answer.*

In this house.

KAROLINA. I've always been here.

ROSE. You're not listed as living here.

KAROLINA. I don't know anything about any listings.

ALEKSANDAR. Is your father here?

> KAROLINA *won't say.*

ROSE. Your father? Is he here?

> KAROLINA *is quiet.*

Listen to me, comrade, you're going to have to talk to us.

KAROLINA *winces*.

MONIKA. Ma'am, please –

KAROLINA (*to* MONIKA). Is this Rose?

MONIKA. Yes.

KAROLINA. She's very beautiful. Let me look at you. My God, you are beautiful.

ROSE. I… Never mind that now. Whether I am or am not beautiful.

KAROLINA. You are.

MONIKA. She is.

ROSE. All right, Comrade Amruš, what are you doing here?

KAROLINA. This is my house.

ROSE. Not any longer it isn't. As an enemy of the people your father has had all his property requisitioned. The house has been assigned to us. That is, a part of the house. The rest will be assigned to another family. Or two. Do you understand?

KAROLINA *nods*.

This house is listed as empty.

KAROLINA. They came a couple of times, some men. Inspecting the house. I hid. There are a couple of convenient nooks in the house. Monika knows.

These gentlemen, comrades, don't seem to know a great deal about architecture.

ROSE. How long have you been here?

KAROLINA. A few months.

ROSE. And where were you before that?

She won't answer.

Comrade –

KAROLINA. You could call me Karolina –

ROSE. We'll get to that later.

Irritable, ROSE *rubs her sore feet.* KAROLINA *registers.* ROSE *is barefoot.*

Where did you come from when you came here?

KAROLINA. From a hospital.

ROSE. Which hospital?

KAROLINA *shakes her head, as if it were an irrelevant piece of information.*

KAROLINA. Vrapče.*

ALEKSANDAR. Oh good, just our luck.

KAROLINA. I assure you I am perfectly sane.

ALEKSANDAR. That entrance a minute ago begs to differ.

ROSE. Hang on. Let's take it step by step. So, you were released from the hospital and you came back here?

ALEKSANDAR. Didn't your father want to take you with him?

KAROLINA. I was not about to go to Argentina! Oh, no. So he could throw me into a hospital over there? I don't dare think what they do to women there. Probably purges and bleeding and cold baths. But he seemed to be in a hurry and he didn't argue much. Well, that was a first.

Silence.

MONIKA. You don't suppose she'd have a right to a part of the house?

ROSE. I don't know. She should go and get registered and she'll find out what rights she has. If she has any. (*Pause.*) We didn't have any, did we? My mother and me. I was two days old. In your big house. We had no rights.

KAROLINA *wilts in her bed. Her face infinitely sad and guilty, she looks at* MONIKA.

KAROLINA. I was all mixed up. I wanted to put it right but then it was too late.

ROSE. You just said you were perfectly fine. So which is it? Are you mixed up or are you not mixed up?

---

* Notorious Croatian mental hospital.

KAROLINA *turns to* ROSE, *like a child, looking at her as if she were an inquisitor.*

MONIKA. Love –

ROSE. Yes, Mother. What?

KAROLINA. It's that you keep being told you're unwell. If you get upset or wish to disagree, every time you abandon equanimity, they say it's your nerves.

ROSE. Who tells you that?

KAROLINA. Everyone. Father, brother, doctors. And after a while you can't be sure. What happened and what didn't happen. Or what's right and what's wrong.

MONIKA *looks at* ROSE, *pleading.*

I came home in the hope that I might die. I have no one. No vocation, no husband, no children and no purpose. So I thought I'd come home, lie down in my bed and attempt to die. I have so far been unsuccessful.

MONIKA. It's a sin what you're saying…

KAROLINA. I suppose you've come to kick me out. I suppose I do deserve that.

MONIKA. We haven't come for that. Have we?

ROSE. We have come to live in an empty house!

KAROLINA *shrugs. In the way of an apology.*

You will have to go to the nearest RIC and register.

KAROLINA. Where?

ROSE. Regional Intelligence Centre. They'll decide where to put you.

MONIKA. What do you mean, where to put her?

ROSE. I'm not sure. She has this… aggravating father circumstance. She'll receive a file. Probably. Have you any useful skills?

KAROLINA. *Bitte? Was für eine –*

ROSE. No, not '*bitte*'. Absolutely not '*bitte*' and the like.

MONIKA. Ma'am, you mustn't speak German.

KAROLINA. I'm sorry. It's when I get nervous. Old habits. I was raised in the Monarchy. German was my first language. I'm sorry.

MONIKA. It's all right, ma'am.

ROSE (*snaps*). Mother, stop calling her 'ma'am'. I mean it. Stop it this instance!

ALEKSANDAR. All right, let's all calm down.

KAROLINA. I can give piano lessons.

ROSE. Piano lessons are not quite as in demand as they used to be.

KAROLINA. That's a shame. Music heals. It lifts the spirit and elevates the character.

ROSE. Listen to me, Comrade Karolina. You are a daughter of a bourgeois Nazi collaborator who escaped being brought to justice. That he would leave you behind in a mental institution only goes to show that he deserves no mercy. However, as he is unavailable to receive punishment, some of our comrades who suffered a great deal under the Nazi boot, might be perfectly happy to take restitution from you. Do you understand? So I suggest you get a grip. I suggest you convince them that the time in the hospital was self-reflective, healing you of all bourgeois convictions and I suggest you think of something socially constructive you are capable of doing with which you might contribute to building the new Yugoslavia.

KAROLINA. I have always strived to contribute. That has been my sole, sole objective since I was a little girl.

ROSE. Excellent. So tomorrow morning you take your release form, go to an RIC and tell them where you were and that, upon release, naturally, you came home.

KAROLINA *drops her gaze.*

What's the matter?

KAROLINA. I can't think where I've put the release form.

ROSE. You must.

KAROLINA. No, it's not coming to me.

ROSE *sighs. She's losing her patience.*

ALEKSANDAR. They gave you a release form, didn't they?

KAROLINA *is quiet.*

When they released you from the hospital?

KAROLINA. Well, it was the end of the war. Mayhem. The doors were open. Nobody paid attention. (*Defensively.*) What would you have done? Stayed there while everyone else left? I was only put in there because it was the easiest thing for my father... I've been inside most of Europe's sanatoriums and thermal spas over the years. Whenever he didn't know what to do with me. Which was often. I'm not crazy.

KAROLINA*'s tone goes up, her heart starts racing, she starts to tremble.*

MONIKA. It's all right. No reason to get upset, is there? You're home now.

ROSE. Mother, this is not her home any more.

KAROLINA. I tried to put things right. No one takes a woman who's been put away seriously. I suppose they're going to put me away again. Because of what he's done. They'll put me away. Somewhere.

KAROLINA *and* MONIKA *clock one another, then both look away and back to* ROSE. *The problem-solver.*

ALEKSANDAR. You could... maybe... ask the General. To put in a good word.

ROSE *winces. She clocks* ALEKSANDAR, *shocked.*

Well, you can't rely on her not to start babbling away... in German... Escaped from a hospital.... You know what they'll do to her?

ROSE. They will assess her case and –

ALEKSANDAR. Rose.

ROSE *considers*.

Rose –

ROSE. What?

KAROLINA. I can sew.

MONIKA. She can. Like a proper tailor. I mean, almost.

ROSE. You can?

KAROLINA. Yes. (*Pause*.) I have a Singer machine.

ALEKSANDAR. You have a Singer machine? In the house?

KAROLINA *points to an object covered with a sheet.*
ALEKSANDAR approaches. He takes the sheet off. A very
well-preserved, 1920s Singer sewing machine makes an
appearance.

Oh, what a beauty. Oh, what a marvellous thing. Look, Rose!

KAROLINA. It's German. As it were. (*To* ALEKSANDAR.)
You know about machines?

ROSE. My husband is a tailor. He works in a factory.

ALEKSANDAR. But with a machine at home, we could set up
a...

His thoughts wander as he inspects the machine with
admiration.

ROSE. We'll see.

ALEKSANDAR (*in check*). Of course. In time. We'll see.

KAROLINA. You could make some clothes for the baby. I have
some fabric in the trunks. You have a little baby, haven't you?

ALEKSANDAR. Yes, we do. So I can use it?

KAROLINA. I suspect you don't have to ask.

ROSE, *quiet, ponders*.

MONIKA. Rose, love –

ROSE. Yes, Mother?

MONIKA. What are we going to do?

ROSE. I don't know.

MONIKA. What about… what Sasha said? About asking the General?

ALEKSANDAR. Damn it, Rose. It's the right… choice.

Silence.

ROSE. Have you anything decent to wear?

KAROLINA. Decent? Yes, I should think so.

ROSE. Something unlike the oil painting.

KAROLINA. Oh. No, I don't think I do.

ROSE. So, the first thing you'll have to do is make some clothes for you. And I'll… see what I can do…

MONIKA *smiles reassuringly at* KAROLINA.

Now I have to check on my… Maša. I have to check on Maša. We should all get some sleep.

ROSE *marches out.* ALEKSANDAR *stays behind. Then he leaves, too. Now* MONIKA *and* KAROLINA *remain alone in the room.* MONIKA *makes her way to the door.*

KAROLINA. What's the matter with her feet?

MONIKA *stops, quiet.* KAROLINA *sits up on her bed. She points to a chair next to it.*

Won't you sit down?

MONIKA *looks to the door, an impulse, unsure.*

Please. Just there. Please.

MONIKA *sits on the chair, perching on the edge. Silence.*

MONIKA. Not much has changed here.

KAROLINA. No.

MONIKA. Except the ivy. It's gone all the way up to the roof. Greener and stronger. Like a blanket.

KAROLINA. Monika. I'm so sorry. I'm so sorry. For my...
impulsive... inexcusable actions.

Silence. They sit a long time in silence.

MONIKA. I figured, if I just turn up at home, with the baby,
they won't have the heart not to let me in. Father wouldn't
look at me. Bringing shame to the house and all. He always
used to say – a woman and a horse need a good thrashing
every three days, just to keep 'em in check. Mother managed
to bring him around. To let me stay.

Rose was a difficult baby. Stubborn like an oil stain. After a
few months, I went to look for work. When she was four my
mother couldn't feed her any more. There was an estate
nearby, needed labourers. They took her for a few years. One
time, they sent her to deliver a telegram – middle of winter –
she walked ten miles through the snow, in her wooden clogs,
no socks. Her little feet almost froze. (*Pause.*) Then I made
up my mind to take her away from there. It took another
couple of years to save up but... I got her back, brought her
to the city. She's terribly bright, you know. She finished
secondary school. And got a job. Not like me, cleaning
houses. A respectable job. In a bank.

She thinks about this for a moment or two as KAROLINA
gazes at her intently.

Once when I was a little girl I got a hold of my brother's
school book. The letters looked like a bunch of little bugs
lined up on the paper. Father caught me looking and beat me.
He called me a time-waster. Rose can make sense of it, you
see. To her they're not bugs on paper. Rosie will think of
something. She's like that. Don't worry.

KAROLINA. Does she know? Does she know what happened?

MONIKA. No... No.

KAROLINA. That's for the best. It would only cause her
trouble nowadays.

Silence.

Monika, it wasn't your fault. Do you understand?

MONIKA. It was a long time ago.

KAROLINA. We'll set it straight.

MONIKA. It's best forgotten, ma'am.

KAROLINA. Perhaps you could call me Karolina.

Scene Seven

January, 1990.

Late evening. Ten thirty on the clock.

The living room – eighties-style. One wall is covered with the popular eighties wallpaper – a forest in the autumn. Brown socialist furniture – a sofa bed and armchairs. In the back, a couple of period pieces from KAROLINA's *youth.*

KARL *and* IGOR, *both in their forties, sit awkwardly on the sofa, smoking, looking at the telly which is conspicuously switched off.* ALISA, *fifteen, sits sulking in the corner.* MARKO, *eighteen, munches on some food. A long table is stacked with food, which* MAŠA *is rearranging.* DUNJA *picks at some fruit.*

VLADO *enters; he joins* KARL *and* IGOR *at the sofa and leans into them.*

VLADO. One–nil.

They look at each other with a silent 'Yes!'

KARL. I was just saying, Vlado, and Alisa here tells me that I am wrong –

ALISA. You are wrong.

KARL. That if we hadn't rushed into the union with the Serbs and the Slovenes we might have had a chance to establish a state of our own back in 1918.

VLADO. She's right, you're wrong.

KARL. I don't think I am.

VLADO. They are doing that bit now at school so she should know.

KARL. Alisa, I wouldn't work too hard on that. Whatever history they're teaching these days, they'll soon change their tune.

ALISA. Sure.

VLADO. She wrote a brilliant essay on Rosa Luxemburg. Alisa, why don't you show Karolina your essay?

ALISA. Surely, Dad, you're not serious.

KAROLINA. Now, Vlado, you must make sure you put away money for her education, I can't stress this enough.

VLADO. Lina, they don't charge for education any more. Have you forgotten?

KARL. I always say, life is the best university.

DUNJA (*to* ALISA). There you see a shining example of that.

LUCIJA *snaps a photo of them.*

VLADO. Be careful, sweetie, you don't want to break it.

LUCIJA. I won't break it.

VLADO. Alisa, can you keep an eye on the camera?

MAŠA. Igor, will you stay the night?

IGOR. Oh, I was thinking I should probably head back home.

DUNJA. To Sarajevo? Tonight? In the snow? It'll take all night.

KARL. What's a little snow going to hurt him?

IGOR. I don't mind. It's a nice drive. I like driving in the night.

KARL. It can be done in five hours, if you know the right route.

IGOR. Maybe not five but –

KARL. I've done it in five plenty of times.

DUNJA. You're a proper Ayrton Senna, aren't you?

MAŠA. Really, in the snow –

IGOR. I have very good heating in my car, it's a new
    Mitsubishi. Excellent value.

VLADO. Yes, the Japanese are not bad these days. Though
    there's nothing like a German car. We have an Audi at the
    moment.

KAROLINA. Would one look at Audi for wheelchairs do you
    think? The engine on mine is on its last legs.

DUNJA. It was the best on the market, Karolina.

KAROLINA. Just goes to show, the Germans are not what they
    used to be.

MAŠA. Igor, you will sleep here. Marko, I'm sure he can sleep
    upstairs at yours. Where's your mother?

MARKO. She took Grandma home.

MAŠA. Right. When will she be back?

MARKO. I… think she'll stay the night. My grandma insists on
    going to funerals but she gets very upset.

KAROLINA. How old is she?

MARKO. Erm… Seventy-two, I think.

KAROLINA. That's young. After about eighty life becomes a
    catalogue of decay. I cannot recommend it to anyone.

MAŠA. Karolina…

IGOR. Erm… I really don't want to impose.

MAŠA. You heard him, he has the flat to himself. He won't
    mind, right?

    MARKO *and* ALISA *exchange a look – their plan just
    ruined.*

MARKO. Of course not… There's plenty of room.

ALISA. I'll go see if I can find that essay.

    She leaves, signalling to MARKO.

DUNJA (*to* IGOR). Stay.

    Like a fine string, a history tightens between them.

IGOR. Well, if I'm not going to drive, I might as well have a drink.

Everyone cheers, except KARL. IGOR *joins* DUNJA *at the table.* MARKO *uses the opportunity to make his excuses.*

MARKO. I'll go and... Look into... sheets and... things...

He slips out of the room.

DUNJA. What would you like?

IGOR. I'll have a whiskey if there's any going.

DUNJA. There is.

KARL. Dunja, is that the one we brought?

DUNJA. Yes, Karl, we brought it.

VLADO. Best German whiskey, eh?

KARL. I'll have one as well. We'll all have a whiskey and the hell with it.

VLADO. Maša, are there any clean glasses –

MAŠA *produces clean glasses, as if by magic.* KARL *joins* DUNJA *and* IGOR, *an awkward trio.* LUCIJA *snaps a photo of the three of them, frozen, sour smiles.* KARL *hovers around the table before going back to the sofa.*

DUNJA. It's nice of you to come.

MAŠA *follows this exchange unobtrusively, but with a keen eye.*

IGOR. Every other day she had me over for lunch. Do you remember?

DUNJA. Good times.

IGOR. The best times.

KARL. How's that whiskey coming along?

DUNJA *snaps out of her moment and pours him a glass.* KARL *drinks it. He heads out of the room, passing* ALEKSANDAR, *seventy-three, at the door.* ALEKSANDAR *walks with a slight limp.*

MAŠA. Daddy, what are you doing up?

ALEKSANDAR. I'm not going to snooze every two hours. I'm not a dog. Where is the dog anyway?

MAŠA. Vlado's colleague has her for the day. You know how she gets with so many people around.

ALEKSANDAR. What people? I don't see any people.

DUNJA. They left, Dad. It's just us now.

MAŠA. Have some Schwarzwald cake.

ALEKSANDAR. I don't want your bourgeois cakes. I want beans. The way Rose made them. With turnips.

MAŠA *screws her face, tears are immediately close to rolling down.*

DUNJA (*forcefully*). Dad, there's no beans. Maša made a feast of delicacies, give it a rest with the beans. Have a smoked-salmon sandwich.

ALEKSANDAR *is quiet, half-sulking, but obeys* DUNJA. *He goes to sit next to* KAROLINA. KAROLINA *puts her hand on his and squeezes it.* MAŠA *assembles some food on a plate for* ALEKSANDAR. KARL *enters. He leans in towards* VLADO.

KARL. One all, motherfuckers.

VLADO. Bloody hell.

MAŠA *looks out the window. She tuts.*

MAŠA. Look at that, back in the garden again. Alisa, Marko, get back in here, do you hear me?

DUNJA. Oh, will you give her some space?

MAŠA. She's not dressed properly, I don't want her ovaries to get it. (*To herself.*) Building a snowman, seriously.

DUNJA. She's fifteen, she's not going to forget not to freeze to death.

MAŠA. Am I supposed not to care?

DUNJA. You're like a python.

Deeply hurt, MAŠA *goes back to meticulously arranging the food.*

VLADO. Maša, what do you think about putting the telly on, see what –

MAŠA. I would be grateful if we could spend this day, in memory of Rose King, without the telly on.

VLADO *and* KARL *exchange a look – 'fuck it' – they gave it a try.*

DUNJA. How's the sandwich, Dad, is it nice?

ALEKSANDAR. It's nice. Soft. Agrees with my teeth. (*To* KAROLINA.) How are you doing, young lady?

KAROLINA. We had thirty-seven pages left. Thirty-seven pages of *Satanic Verses*.

ALEKSANDAR. I could come and take over the reading. My sight is pretty good you know.

KAROLINA. I know it is. It's your snoozing I'm worried about.

VLADO. Maša, did I tell you Stevo rang earlier?

MAŠA. From Dubai?

VLADO. Yes. To offer his condolences.

MAŠA. All the way from Dubai. That's nice of him.

KARL. Stevo. He's that Serbian pal of yours.

VLADO. Been mates since the army days. He's invited us over again.

MAŠA. Has he.

VLADO. Yes. (*To everyone*.) He's relocated to Dubai, flying for this airline, what's it called –

MAŠA. Emirates.

VLADO. Emirates. He says, they live like kings over there. And we keep thinking, we should go, but we keep coming up short – it's never the right time –

IGOR. Well, I tell you what, in another few months, a year at the most, our little bungalow in Dalmatia will be finished. You're all welcome there. Summer of '92 at the latest.

DUNJA. That would be wonderful.

IGOR. It's not Dubai, but you can't beat our good old coast.

KARL. If we're all alive and well by '92. You see what's going on.

IGOR. It will settle down eventually.

KARL. One way or another.

IGOR. What do you mean?

KARL. You know, you keep going on about things, like you had no eyes or ears.

VLADO. Ah, Karl, you and your ideas –

KARL. Nothing wrong with my ideas. You should reconsider your ideas is what you should do. You've got equality coming out of your arse, but you keep coming up short.

VLADO. So what do you propose?

KARL. This house, for example. You should own it. All of it.

VLADO. What would we do with the whole house? And where in the hell would everybody else go and live? It's been forty-five years. I'd like to see you bring that up with Horaks the Horrible downstairs. They kick up a fuss about something every five minutes. That poor snowman is going to get it before long.

KARL. But the house does not belong to them, does it?

VLADO. It doesn't belong to anyone, or in fact it belongs to everyone. That's the whole point of nationalisation!

KARL. The point is wrong! The house was built and paid for by Karolina's family. She should own it. And since she is practically family and has no heirs, and her brother, what was his name –

KAROLINA (*quietly*). Sebastian.

KARL. Sebastian. Since Sebastian perished in what was it, some drunken brawl in...

KAROLINA. Pécs –

KARL. Pécs, who would she leave it to –

KAROLINA. Not you, I shouldn't think –

KARL. I don't mean me. I'm talking about the principle and we can't even talk about the principle of the matter, only because we're not allowed to mention her late father since everyone who fought for the Croatian cause has been branded a monster –

IGOR. They were Nazi collaborators –

KARL. It's not all so black and white –

VLADO. How is that not black and white – either you sided with the Germans or you sided against them –

MAŠA (*defensively*). There were also the Croatian Guard soldiers* – they didn't side with anyone, they were just drafted –

VLADO. I'm not talking about the Croatian Guard, who's talking about the Croatian Guard –

He inadvertently turns to ALEKSANDAR.

MAŠA. I'm just saying, they had no choice –

VLADO. I know they had no choice, nobody's saying otherwise. But Karolina's father wasn't drafted – he was a politician – and he chose Hitler.

KARL. He built this house from the ground up with his own hands.

KAROLINA. Well –

KARL. Funds. Private property should belong to the person, regardless of character or political views.

VLADO. That is a moral and political fallacy.

KAROLINA. He certainly wouldn't get points on character.

---

* The Croatian Home Guard was founded in April 1941, a few days after the founding of the Independent State of Croatia (NDH) itself, following the collapse of the Kingdom of Yugoslavia. It was done with the authorisation of German occupation authorities.

LUCIJA (*to* MAŠA, *quietly*). He chose Hitler?

MAŠA. Erm, in a way... Don't say that at school.

VLADO. You see, sweetie, our people, a section of our people has always wanted independence. A state of our own.

KARL. A significant portion.

LUCIJA. Yugoslavian people?

VLADO. No, sweetie, Croatian people.

LUCIJA. And we are Croatian.

VLADO. Yes, we are.

KARL. She doesn't know she's Croatian?

DUNJA. Ah, Karl, please –

VLADO. She knows. But we are also Yugoslavian.

KARL. What does that even mean? It doesn't even exist. It's an invention.

VLADO. Technically, all nation states are an invention.

KARL. Not true.

DUNJA. You tell him. You tell the man, a historian, what is and isn't true.

KARL. Well, I will. Shall I tell you why? Because all our historical figures have been disfigured for the Communist agenda and they've deformed our sense of nationhood, made us feel ashamed of ourselves.

IGOR. Ustaše* is not something to be proud of.

KARL. The partisans were no angels either.

VLADO. There's no comparison. Please, Karl. Where would the world be today without our partisans and the Red Army? What would Germany be like today? You think they'd have you there?

KARL. All, I'm saying is, it's not all quite the way we have been led to believe the past forty-five years. I was told this by one of our people in Düsseldorf, a guy who knows just about all there is to know about our history.

---

* Ustaše were a radical Croatian nationalist organisation aligned with the Nazi forces in WWII, they were responsible for numerous atrocities committed against Serbs, Jews and Croatian Communists.

VLADO. Actually, it's now that the revisionism is starting. Now, all of a sudden, martyrs start popping up and every other two-bit political opportunist is suddenly a hero of the national cause. You have to keep your objective head on, you know.

KARL. Cos you're objective. You think a system is like a heart condition – you're born with it and you die of it. But it's not. Things change. Governments fall. Wars break out.

MAŠA. Christ, Karl, what are you on about? Governments fall? Wars break out? We'd have no country left.

KARL. Yes we would. We'd have Croatia.

MAŠA. But we wouldn't have Yugoslavia.

KARL. What the hell do we need Yugoslavia for? What use have you got from it?

MAŠA. 'What use'? What do you mean, 'what use'?

KARL. A country is supposed to be of use to its people. It's a lesson you learn in capitalism. Aleksandar, you must understand what I mean.

ALEKSANDAR *raises his head from his sandwich; he is not following this conversation.*

You started a little tailoring business at home, alongside your job, way back, when was it?

DUNJA. It wasn't a business, it was making ends meet.

KARL. You had a good capitalist brain on you. You knew what it took to look after your family.

ALEKSANDAR (*alarmed*). What is he trying to say?

VLADO (*protectively*). Nothing. He isn't trying to say anything. Karl, we're safer here than you are in capitalism.

KARL. Well, time will tell.

DUNJA. Karl has become an expert on politics. And he has developed a passion for our history, haven't you? Our Croatian history, that is.

KARL. Our people in Germany are saying there's going to be a war.

DUNJA. Who is saying that?

MAŠA. Among us? I don't believe it.

DUNJA (*to* KARL). Who are these 'our people in Germany'?

KARL (*to* MAŠA). 'Us'? Who is 'us'?

MAŠA. The Croats. And the Serbs. And the Slovenians.

KARL. Leave the Slovenians out of it.

IGOR. What about the Bosnians?

KARL. Oh, you're screwed. To hell and back.

ALEKSANDAR. My Rose thought there was going to be a war. She said to me, I do not intend to live just long enough to lose the country I fought for when I was young, she said. And she fought, like a tiger, my Rose.

KAROLINA *strokes his face.*

KARL. A conflict is inevitable. The only surprising thing is that we kept it together for this long after Tito's death. But it will break.

DUNJA. If the shit hits the fan –

KARL. When. When.

DUNJA. If and when the shit hits the fan, I want you to send the girls to ours in Düsseldorf.

LUCIJA. Mum?

VLADO. Dunja, let's not get carried away.

DUNJA. I'm just saying, so you know, that's all. And your boy, Igor.

IGOR. Dunja, the way we're all mixed in Bosnia, God and Allah couldn't untangle us if they rolled up their sleeves and worked together.

DUNJA *smiles. Tenderly.* LUCIJA *sits down next to* ALEKSANDAR. *She pushes her photographs into his hands. He puts his arm around* LUCIJA.

DUNJA. Just saying. Isn't that right, Karl? We'd take the kids.

KARL. If we're there.

DUNJA. Where else would we be?

KARL. Someone's going to have to defend the country.

MAŠA. Defend the country?

KARL. From the Serbs for fuck's sake!

VLADO. It won't come to that –

KARL. Are you blind?! Can't you see they've been strategically positioning themselves all over the world? What do you think that Stevo geezer is doing in Dubai? Counting sand? Riding camels?

VLADO (*laughing*). You crack me up, seriously. My Stevo, strategically positioned?

He goes on laughing, which irritates KARL.

ALEKSANDAR. No more strategic positioning. That's exactly what the Major said. Run for your lives.

MAŠA. What are you saying, Dad?

ALEKSANDAR. We used to have some pictures. Mashenka, where did we... Oh, I remember. We had them and then Rose burnt them. She burnt all the pictures with me wearing the uniform.

MAŠA. Dad?

ALEKSANDAR. Such were the times. Best not to have things to remember them by.

KAROLINA. It doesn't stop us remembering.

ALEKSANDAR. It doesn't stop me seeing her when I close my eyes. My Dolly.

VLADO. Who's Dolly, Sasha?

ALEKSANDAR. My white mare. I see her tied to that tree with her crazed eyes.

MAŠA. Dad, what are you on about?

DUNJA. Let him talk. I don't see why everyone should be allowed to babble on, but Dad ought to be quiet.

ALEKSANDAR. He rounded us up, our Major, in the barracks in Zagreb. May, 1945. The partisans have won the war. And he says to us: all right, Croatian guards, those of you who have a change of clothes, leave your uniforms and make a run for it, try and reach your homes and your lands. When you come face to face with the partisans – tell them, you did not kill, you did not pillage and burn, you are not murderers and thieves. You're not Ustaše, you're soldiers. You were drafted by what was then an official authority. And hopefully you'll be spared. And you, Ustaše, a change of clothes if you have any, if not, you better pray to God and pray hard!

LUCIJA. Why must they pray?

MAŠA. Shush. I'll tell you later.

ALEKSANDAR. So I get home to my village. Rose is gone, they say she joined the partisans, went to the woods, nobody knows more. And the people in the village, the few people in the village, they tell me, you better run for it, what do the partisans care, if you're not with them, you're against them. So I take Dolly. I'm thinking I'll have some company. And she was so happy to see me, how was I going to leave her again? And off we go, towards Slovenia, where people went. People like me. I get there, there's a sea of men. The word was, we cross the border into Austria, surrender to the English and we'll be safe. But the route is steep, through the mountain, up some goat paths through the rocks. I can't take her along. I tie her to a tree, I'm thinking, someone will come and take her – a true beauty she was, white and proud, with only a few grey flecks. And I tie her to a tree… I tie her to a… tree and I leave her. Two days and two nights we walked across the mountain. No food or drink. After two days the word spreads – the English have refused to take us. We must walk back and surrender to the partisans. The partisans make us march back through Croatia to Serbia. Long, long lines of people walking, with the partisans on each side. You don't know if they'll spit on you or shoot you. And then I see Dolly – still tied to that tree. Only different. Wide-eyed, scared out of her wits. She'd gnawed the bark of the tree. Her mouth all cuts and blood. And she sees me – I swear, her eyes clear up – and she tries to break off, she almost strangles herself. My heart wants to break, I take a step out of the line, a couple of men in the line, they pull me back at the last moment, just as one of the partisans has reached for his gun... And we continue in the line. She stays behind. She stays behind alone.

Silence.

DUNJA. And you?

ALEKSANDAR. I keep walking. Six hundred kilometres. To a camp. My Rose finds me there. She takes me out of the camp. She saves my life.

Silence. MAŠA *embraces* ALEKSANDAR *from behind. He squeezes her hand, his eyes moist.*

DUNJA. Look at the two of you, Daddy.

ALEKSANDAR. What?

DUNJA. Look at you and Maša. Spitting image.

ALEKSANDAR. You reckon? Do you really reckon?

He wraps his arms around her. MAŠA *wipes her eyes and her nose.*

MAŠA. Vlado, turn the telly on. See what Red Star's doing?

VLADO. What do you mean?

MAŠA. Oh, just turn it on. You're missing the evening news by the way.

VLADO. Bloody hell.

VLADO hurriedly turns the telly on. The iconic sound of the Yugoslavian news programme comes on. Archive footage – the 14th congress of the Central Committee of Yugoslavia.

VOICE OF THE PRESENTER. On the third day of the session of the 14th congress of the Central Committee of Yugoslavia in Belgrade, the committee members have voted against the amendments proposed by the Slovenian delegation. The amendments called for a confederalisation of the Party and the State, which would ensure greater autonomy for all Yugoslavian republics. In an unprecedented move, the Slovenian delegation has left the congress.

VLADO. They've left the congress! Slovenians have left the congress!

MAŠA. They can't leave the congress. That's not... done!

Everyone stares at the news, transfixed.

VOICE OF THE PRESENTER. The head of the Croatian delegation, Comrade Ivica Račan, proposed a recess until this newly formed situation is resolved noting that a further session without one of the republic delegations would not be in keeping with the Yugoslavian character of the Party and could not be considered legitimate. Comrade Slobodan Milošević called for the congress to be continued regardless of the absence of the Slovenian delegation. Having their proposition turned down, as a sign of protest, the Croatian delegation has also left the congress –

VLADO (*stunned*). They're leaving! We're leaving! We've left!

VOICE OF THE PRESENTER. Thus effectively ending the 14th congress of the Central Committee of the Communist Union of Yugoslavia.

IGOR. Shit.

KAROLINA. So it goes.

MAŠA. But that means...

Silence.

IGOR. Yugoslavia's fucked.

Scene Eight

November, 2011.

After midnight.

ALISA, *thirty-six, walks into the dining room, carrying a bottle of whiskey. She finds* LUCIJA, *thirty-three, in her pyjamas, at the table, eating the apple cake from the tray. An old trunk is pushed to the side of the room.*

ALISA. What are you doing?

LUCIJA. Couldn't sleep.

ALISA. Nervous?

LUCIJA. Hungry. I haven't eaten properly in a week.

    ALISA *sits at the table, pours herself a drink.*

ALISA. You haven't eaten properly in a decade.

LUCIJA. Not true. I had a very indulgent Sunday lunch in 2007. What about you?

ALISA. Can't sleep either. (*Re: the trunk.*) Where did that come from?

LUCIJA. The attic. Everyone seems to think that old crap from every nook and cranny in the house should be dumped on me to deal with.

ALISA. That ought to give you a pleasant sense of entitlement.

    LUCIJA *keeps eating.* ALISA *opens the trunk and pulls out an old, early-twentieth-century lady's dress.*

LUCIJA. Karolina's?

ALISA. Too fancy to be Great-Grandma's? I think it's the one in the portrait.

    ALISA *brings the dress to her face and inhales the smell.*

Smells like history. Put it on.

LUCIJA. No. You think?

    LUCIJA *undresses and carefully puts on the dress. It's too tight across her chest and altogether a size too small.*

People were smaller a hundred years ago.

ALISA. Certainly in the chest area.

LUCIJA. Congratulations. It's been all of six hours before you started giving me shit.

ALISA raises her hands in a conciliatory manner.

It's easy for you to judge. Having not taken after the fat side of the family. Do you know that breasts are made of fat? You lose the fat, you lose the breasts. Or keep both. What kind of a Sophie's Choice is that?

ALISA. So, Sophie lost the fat and put on a pair of wedding breasts.

LUCIJA. I didn't put them on you, did I?

ALISA approaches LUCIJA and starts buttoning up the dress at the back. LUCIJA pulls her belly in and inhales as ALISA straps her into the dress.

ALISA. 'Fooling around doesn't mean you're gay'?

She pulls the dress tighter. LUCIJA can barely breathe.

LUCIJA. I've done things. I might even have done things you haven't.

ALISA. Do tell.

LUCIJA. No.

Some buttons snap open.

Oh, shit.

They giggle.

No more cake for me.

ALISA laughs.

ALISA. I've missed you.

LUCIJA. I've missed you too. Freak. 'Koala bear.'

ALISA has put on a period coat and hat. LUCIJA produces a small bag of pot, rolling papers and cigarettes from her handbag. She starts rolling a spliff.

You know I had my first spliff with Karolina?

ALISA. What?

LUCIJA. When Grandma Rose died, I landed the exciting task of going to the home to read to Karolina. She thought she was instilling a reading habit in me.

ALISA. You used to love going there.

ALISA *comes to sit at the table, in the coat and the hat.*

LUCIJA. No, I used to love getting paid in chocolate. Grandma Rose used to come and read, but you know how she'd start lecturing on Tito and the Party as soon as she had an audience. So when I got there and just read, they loved me! Those were the years I got really fat. Then Karolina discovered dope. There was that old hippy in the home, who was growing it on the balcony. If she hadn't died soon after I would have turned into an elephant!

LUCIJA *hands* ALISA *the spliff. She lights it.*

Why is it wrong to feel entitled?

ALISA. Because reading to and taking drugs with an old bat doesn't entitle you to her house.

The spliff travels back and forth from ALISA *to* LUCIJA.

LUCIJA. It's not that! We have a history here. Four generations.

ALISA. Okay, yes. We do. Let's call it continuity. This is a beautiful thing, nostalgic, sentimental, in a good way. But it doesn't give you a sacred right to the bricks and the land over the other people who also live here. The transition-born aristocracy you've joined is a very different thing. You're not protecting our heirloom.

LUCIJA. I think that *is* what I'm doing.

She smiles a knowing smile.

ALISA. How?

LUCIJA. Karolina told me, she said, all of this should be mine.

ALISA. Yours, alone?

LUCIJA. She said, yours. I'm not sure if she meant singular or plural. But she said it. Why would she say that?

ALISA. Because she was high! And old and crazy. Maybe she was afraid her dad had more children in Argentina and they might come for their inheritance.

LUCIJA. Before she died, Karolina asked Mum and Dad to help her find a lawyer. To write a will. I remember, she said it was important. But it was in the middle of the war. Dad had just lost his job. Dunja was moving in with us. They were overwhelmed. Nobody had time for her. And then she died. We never thought Karolina would actually die one day.

ALISA. Okay. It's possible she would have said she wanted us to have the house – which at that point wasn't even hers to give. But it's equally possible she would have left her earthly possessions to a dog shelter –

LUCIJA. Please! You know there were always things not talked about.

ALISA. Because her father was a Nazi. And because she'd been in an asylum. Those were sensitive matters.

LUCIJA. What if she'd been put away because she got pregnant out of wedlock.

ALISA. What?!

LUCIJA. Couldn't keep the child so had a maid look after it...

ALISA. Had a maid... I will not have you renouncing Great-Grandma Monika and our background!

LUCIJA. All I'm saying is it's possible she would have revealed in the will things that she was too traumatised to talk about.

ALISA. Why would she kick Monika out with the baby then?

LUCIJA. I don't know because nobody thought to get to the bottom of it when it was time –

ALISA. You can't use an imaginary will to justify a claim to the house!

LUCIJA. Who in their right mind could be so against getting a house?

ALISA. I can't get my head around it. I have never in a million years thought the whole house would be ours. We never aspired to it... It was never even a value to... value.

LUCIJA. A value to value. Impressive.

ALISA (*putting the spliff out*). This is strong.

LUCIJA. Do you share these ideas around in England? About how private property is not a value to value? I'm sure they love you, you old socialist.

ALISA. Well, actually, England has a long tradition of socialist –

LUCIJA. What?

ALISA. Thought.

LUCIJA. '*Socialist thought*'! First of all, it wasn't a value to value because it wasn't done. Second of all, we were poor, Alisa! Without Dunja's German stash we would have starved when Dad got fired from the school. You know, providing a house for your family to live in is an honourable thing.

ALISA. Dad got fired because he was honourable. I don't get this personality U-turn you've taken!

LUCIJA. It's not a U-turn. You just want everything to stay the same, so you could feel cosy and familiar when you grace us with your presence.

ALISA. I don't expect everything to stay the same, I just expect that things don't reverse to where they were however the hell long ago when the rich were rich and the poor were poor and a little bit embarrassing to be seen with. And women were there to be pretty and perfect. No, I don't like the change. That you're suddenly taking the sacraments, and having pre-wedding cosmetic surgery and that we'll be doing the 'Buy the Bride' fucking peasant ritual that not even Grandma Rose gave a shit about fifty years ago!

LUCIJA. How can you be so judgemental? You make the weirdest choices of your own and you don't see me judging you!

ALISA. The choices I make, I make for myself. You make yours for other people.

LUCIJA. I choose to make that choice!

ALISA. That's a bullshit argument. Freedom of choice doesn't mean every choice is equally valid.

LUCIJA. I can't wait for you to come back one day and start administering all your wisdom to this backward nation.

ALISA. I'm thinking about it!

Beat. LUCIJA *is taken aback*.

LUCIJA. You are?

ALISA. I don't know. Maybe.

Pause.

LUCIJA. To live with us?

ALISA. Perhaps. (*Pause*.) Perhaps in the country. In the nature. Away from the city.

LUCIJA. Fuck me. Male, female, east, west, town, country. You really are mixed up. (*Laughs*.) Well, if you decide to come back, you can have the attic. (*Beat*.) We can do it up for you.

ALISA *takes it in*.

Dad would pee his pants with joy if you came back.

They both burst out laughing. The spliff has kicked in.

Remember the Polaroid camera Dunja brought from Germany? Dad took about twenty pictures of you. The single one he took of me, he also managed to get the dog taking a crap in the background.

More laughter. The clock strikes one. LUCIJA *gets up*.

I'm going to bed. Have to be pretty and perfect tomorrow. I might throw up first.

ALISA. Great idea. (*Pause*.) Look. I'm sorry. I don't mean to be… unsupportive.

LUCIJA. You know, Damjan is not a bad guy. I wish you'd keep an open mind.

LUCIJA *kisses* ALISA *on the top of the head. She grabs a mouthful of cake from the tray. She makes her way out, and then stops*.

Is that what you were going to announce at dinner? That you were coming home?

ALISA. Oh. No. No, I wasn't. I was going to toast you. That's all.

LUCIJA. Right. Goodnight.

She leaves. Screeching noise comes from upstairs.

Scene Nine

January, 1990.

The garden. ALISA, *fifteen, and* MARKO, *eighteen, stand facing each other, in the snow.*

MARKO. It's only a year.

ALISA. It's a whole year. What's there to do in the army for a whole year?

MARKO. Will you come visit?

ALISA. Where will you go, do you know?

MARKO. Bosnia. Mostar.

ALISA *is quiet.*

ALISA. Girlfriends come to visit.

MARKO. Well… good girlfriends.

ALISA *looks up to meet his eyes. She giggles, breaking eye contact and throws a snowball at him. She runs, he chases her.*

They kiss. The pristine first snow falls on them. It's a pretty night, like a fairytale.

Scene Ten

January, 1990.

The living room, after midnight.

Everyone has gone to bed. DUNJA *and* KARL *are getting ready for bed. A sofa bed has been made up for them. Their luggage is open on the floor.* DUNJA *is sorting out her toiletries.* KARL *sits on the sofa bed, quiet, thoughtful, drunk. As she passes by him up and down, the silence between them becomes palpable.*

DUNJA. Are you not speaking to me?

> KARL *unbuttons his shirt in silence.*

> So we're not speaking. Fine by me. There are certainly greater tragedies going on today than you not speaking to me.

> *She takes off her blouse. The clock strikes one.*

> *Silence goes on for a bit. He pours himself another drink.* DUNJA *would love to give him a hard time about it, but she can't, as they're not speaking to each other.*

KARL. You care about them more than you care about me.

DUNJA. Spare me, Karl.

KARL. 'Spare me, Karl.' Can you think of a single other expression than that?

> *She rolls her eyes.*

> That, yes, that one right there. Huh?

DUNJA. What do you want from me? My mum just died, you idiot, the country's just fallen apart. Give me a break!

> *She takes her skirt off and remains in a nice, white-silk negligee, good German quality.*

KARL. Inviting people to come and stay, send their children... Taking in your boyfriend's children –

DUNJA. You start that again, I swear my head is going to explode...

KARL. All the decent people left when it was time to leave, but not Igor, oh no. Hanging around until it's too late to leave. It's so cheap it's embarrassing.

DUNJA. Yes, he's cheap. 'Did we bring this whiskey?' Did we pay for it? Is it us who have the cash for shit you guys can't afford?

KARL. He's drinking my whiskey and preying on my wife –

DUNJA. Karl, he is a friend of the family. Rose was like a mother to him. I told you this a million times. He was as poor as a church mouse and Rose watched over him so he could finish his studies and not starve. And now that she's dead, you could allow the man a little bit of leeway to mourn her. Even if it means fucking staying the night. One floor up from a married woman he used to like a little, twenty years ago.

KARL. I just want to be consulted, it's not too much to ask –

DUNJA. If there's a war, we'll take the kids, do I have to ask your permission?

KARL. Of course we'll take the damn kids. That's not the point.

DUNJA. What is the point?

KARL. The point is how it looks to other people when you treat me like I'm not even worth consulting. Like my say has no weight. 'Napoleon complex.' A fifteen-year-old tells me I have a Napoleon complex.

DUNJA. Karl, you're drunk.

KARL. I am sick and tired of being a nobody – I will not do it any more –

DUNJA. You're not a nobody. You run a company, for God's sake, you live a free life in a capitalist system, which you so worship. Every time you come back in your car and your suits, with your whiskeys everyone you know turns green –

KARL. You run a company. All I am is… is…

DUNJA. Company Director.

KARL. Nominally. Everybody knows you're the boss. They're all laughing at me behind my back.

DUNJA. Nobody's laughing at you. Don't be stupid.

KARL. We'll always be scum over there. Balkans. Yugoslavs. Gastarbeiters.

DUNJA. Gastarbeiters live in shacks and dig ditches. We live in the suburbs, we have a house and two cars, we're about to build a pool!

KARL. There comes a time when a man feels like returning to his – fatherland. To give back to his people and country. To be Someone.

DUNJA. So now, when you claim the war is about to break out, now you want to come back.

KARL. Croatia is going to have to be 'made', don't you understand? Don't you see these people around you? They haven't got a fucking clue!

DUNJA. You are going to 'make' Croatia?

KARL. Why not? Am I a retard? Am I incapable of taking initiative?

DUNJA. Do you really think that… Ah, you're losing the plot.

KARL. I'm losing the plot – will you listen to me – it's so fucking infuriating talking to you. This, all this, which you all thought was for all eternity, all of this is going to pieces. And if we don't get ready, the Serbs are going to exterminate us.

DUNJA. And what do you propose? Marching into battle?

KARL. If need be. I know, it's not something one plans for in life, but if it comes to that… yes… take a rifle and… and… fight.

DUNJA. You were taken out of serving the army with a doctor's note. You couldn't take the pressure back in the day when peace was as stable as a bar of fucking gold. You can't string together two days without drink. You haven't so much as ran to catch a bus in twenty years, you sweat through every time you have to negotiate a contract. You are going to march ahead and defend our country. Well, I feel safe.

KARL. What a cunt you are.

Long silence. Rage festers in KARL as he gets another drink.

DUNJA. Karl, we should think about splitting up. I can't say that I love you any more. I've certainly lost respect for you. And you annoy the hell out of me. Let's cut our losses and separate like, you know, normal people.

KARL stares at her, stunned. He looks away.

KARL. I was thinking we should renew the vows. Do it in church this time.

DUNJA. What?

He's not kidding. DUNJA stares at him. Then she laughs.

You have lost your mind, you well and truly have.

And she laughs some more. KARL watches her laugh, he drinks up his drink. She's laughing. KARL strikes her. Across the face, in a 'manly' fashion as they say. Blood spurts out from her lip.

DUNJA goes quiet momentarily, stunned. Then a sound comes out of her mouth – a defensive, shocked sound that sounds like laughter. KARL strikes her again. She falls on the floor knocking over a vase and some dishes. The blood is now sprayed over her white negligee. He strikes her a few more times. She screams. He pulls her hair and clenches his fist, he stares into her eyes and her face covered in blood and the clenched fist is a second away from landing in her face – VLADO and MAŠA tumble into the room.

VLADO. What the –

KARL lets DUNJA go. He stands towering above her.

MAŠA. Jesus Christ.

KARL, himself stunned, takes a few steps back. MAŠA runs to DUNJA, drops to the floor and gently embraces her. DUNJA sits on the floor, shaking.

VLADO stares at the scene. ALISA and MARKO run into the room. LUCIJA behind them. She stares in shock.

ALISA. Oh, my God.

MAŠA. What have you done to her?

   KARL *drops on the bed and begins to cry.*

VLADO. I'm going to call an ambulance.

Scene Eleven

November, 2011.

Outside the house. Two o'clock.

MARKO, *thirty-nine, is stacking a couple of large boxes.*
ALISA, *thirty-six, appears at the door.*

ALISA. Hey there, Mister Muscle!

   He drops the boxes, startled.

MARKO. Hey.

   *A moment of uncertainty before he embraces her. She holds
the half-smoked spliff in her hand.*

   Tough night at the Kos family?

ALISA. I confiscated it from my baby sister. Can I interest you?

MARKO. No, I don't really go for that any more. PTSD and
   THC – apparently – are not friends. I beg to differ but I'm
   assured there's a lot of research…

ALISA. Oh. Of course.

MARKO. I thought you'd be here sooner.

ALISA. For the circus? I had to work.

MARKO. Ah, yes. Teaching at a college. I heard.

ALISA. I give lectures, as part of my PhD. It's not quite as
   glamorous as Dad makes it sound.

MARKO. Oh, I don't know. Invention of photography – the seminal shift in self-perception in women? Sounds pretty up there.

ALISA. My own mentor couldn't memorise the title.

MARKO. What can I say, I'm a fan.

Beat. An awkward smile between them.

ALISA. The crazy English, you know, they expect teachers to show up for class.

MARKO. You don't say?

ALISA. A hen night doesn't seem to count as legitimate absence?!

MARKO. The mind boggles.

ALISA. Had I known…

MARKO. You never would have left.

ALISA. Never.

MARKO. If we had this wisdom and that age –

ALISA. Oh, I think I'd be unbearable.

MARKO. Even more unbearable.

She smiles. Pause.

ALISA. I'm sorry.

MARKO *takes it in.*

I could have been more patient. I shouldn't have run away.

MARKO.…Oh… you mean back then?

ALISA. Yes. What do you mean?

He looks at her, searching.

MARKO. Right. You've nothing to be sorry for. I'm the one who's sorry. I was a mess and you were right to leave.

ALISA. I sometimes wonder –

MARKO. So do I.

Pause.

ALISA. It's odd to see you go.

MARKO takes another long, intent look at ALISA.

MARKO. Yeah. (*Pause.*) Yeah. Well, you know, pushing forty, moving out. They say I'm reckless but my mind is made up.

ALISA giggles.

ALISA. When we were kids, I always hoped the Horaks would move away and we magically had the house for just you and us.

MARKO. It turns out the house is only for the Kos's.

ALISA. I don't understand this at all. My sister has become the high priestess of tradition.

MARKO. I'm not sure tradition is what you'd call it.

ALISA. What would you call it?

MARKO. Oh… you wouldn't like what I'd call it.

Pause. She scrutinises him.

(*Changing the subject.*) How long are you staying?

ALISA. …I don't know. I thought… I'd stay for a while.

MARKO. Like a longer while?

ALISA. Yeah. Maybe. I'm just a… I kind of need to figure out things so. I thought I'd do that at home.

MARKO. Right. Right. Great.

ALISA. So where are you headed?

MARKO. Mum is going to Dalmatia, to live with my sister. And I'm off to one of those high-rise new-builds if you can imagine.

ALISA. A high-rise bachelor's pad. Aren't you going to be a catch?

MARKO. Yes. It might not be a bachelor pad. (*Pause.*) I've been seeing someone for a while. We've talked about it. I thought I might give living with someone other than Mum a shot. An experiment.

ALISA. Of course. How wonderful. Of course.

MARKO. We'll see. She seems to know what she's doing. And you? Last time I think there was a... Portuguese man?

ALISA. Oh, yeah. That. The painter. That didn't... you know... There was a brief French connection...

MARKO. Testing the EU on our behalf?

ALISA. Yes. A couple of Serbs spoil the average.

MARKO laughs. She puts the spliff out.

Are you guys going to be making music all night? It's two o'clock.

MARKO. Oh. No. I think we're done.

She heads inside. MARKO picks up a key from a box.

By the way, I found this in the attic. I think it's the old key to the house. Give it to Lucy. A wedding present so to speak. To the mistress of the house.

Beat. ALISA takes the key.

ALISA. Are you... I'm presuming you're not coming to the wedding.

MARKO. No, we're not.

ALISA. I was hoping to have an ally there.

MARKO. Alisa, for fuck's sake, I'm not your ally in this.

ALISA (*taken aback*). I'm sorry?

MARKO. I wish you'd lose this deer-in-the-headlights look – it really isn't your thing.

He stops. She stares at him. A long pause, his face screwed in reluctance – he does not want to enter into this speech. But then... here it goes:

What I'm saying is that... I can't... There is a line to which you can be stretched. There is a line.

ALISA. Okay...

He takes another moment to weigh it out.

MARKO. Stuff has happened between us in the past. We have been very grown-up and cordial about it all because, ultimately, what transpired was not out of ill-feeling or… the bullshit that goes on between people when a relationship starts breaking down. But… if we were to unpick the layers of let's call it social conditioning and all this jovial 'it's all in the past' approach to things, I think we would find that what happened years ago, what I put you through in those months after I came back from the front line was pretty fucking grim. And there are probably consequences of that somewhere in your life. I carry my guilt around with me for messing it all up. And for putting my mother and sister through years of worry. Three years of was I going to come home at all. And then was I going to live a normal life, or take my own, or someone else's, or theirs, or whatever the fuck… you know. But here's the kicker. Whilst I was sitting around trying to grasp how anyone can just get on with life after that monumental bloodbath, I missed out on acquiring the necessary skills to live in the new world. The years spent scratching my head about the, now largely forgotten attempt to protect my country, which wasn't even my choice, have rendered me unable to protect my own doorstep and my own mother from being evicted at the age of seventy-two.

You know what he said, your brother-in-law? 'Let's talk man to man.' Huh. Well. Our flat is seriously run-down and I'd never get the money to fix it. So I rolled over really quite promptly after he explained to me that refusing the offer would not be an option. The hateful Horaks, they at least put up a little of a fight. I have more respect for them than I have for myself right now. So. You know. I screwed up many, many things. And this inclination that you still seem to have towards me I find pathetically moving. But a line has been crossed. I can't sit in the back of the restaurant with you, drink their champagne and scoff quietly. Contempt is a very poor weapon. I am not your ally. Any more.

ALISA *stares at him.* MARKO *leaves.* ALISA *remains on her own.*

Scene Twelve

November, 2011.

Three o'clock. Darkness.

MAŠA *and* VLADO*'s bedroom* (KAROLINA*'s old bedroom*).

VLADO, *sixty-seven, snores.* MAŠA, *sixty-six, turns a lamp on. She opens a drawer in her bedside table and pulls out some photographs. She goes through them.*

MAŠA. Are you asleep, Vlado?

> VLADO *grunts.*

> Are you asleep?

VLADO. Not any more I'm not.

MAŠA. How can you sleep, anyway?

VLADO. Is that one of those questions where I'm screwed whatever I say?

MAŠA. What? No. I'm just thinking…

VLADO. Don't think. Get some sleep. I barely got any and it will be a long day.

MAŠA. What were you thinking about?

VLADO. I wasn't thinking. I had heartburn.

MAŠA. Well I'm thinking. About Tatiana.

VLADO (*now fully awake*). Bloody hell, what kind of a leap is that? Must I spend my whole life proving to you –

MAŠA. Oh, shush. You have an annoying habit of jumping to conclusions.

VLADO. What then?

MAŠA. I'm thinking – what would your life have been like if you hadn't met me and married her. With all that wealth she made…

VLADO. I was lucky to get out alive. She has buried two husbands since then.

MAŠA. Okay, but, if you'd made different decisions. If you'd
been more politically strategic in '91… That idiot they
replaced you with at school ended up advising on education.

VLADO. You can't be strategic if you're not strategic. You
can't go against your conscience.

MAŠA. I know.

VLADO. I'm not sorry. I look back and I'm not sorry, Maša. I
can look myself in the mirror, I don't have to pretend that
time never happened. Like many others. 'In the war,
different rules apply.' No, they don't. The only thing that
happens in the war is that you get used to it. It becomes the
new normal and you lose sight of the fact that one day it will
pass, one day the real normal is going to come back and you
will have to account for those savage, ruthless, self-serving
traits, which got the better of you.

MAŠA. And this is why I always admired you.

VLADO. Did you? Inconspicuously I must say.

MAŠA. No, I did. And I do.

VLADO. And yet I find you awake in the middle of the night
considering where you made the wrong turn.

MAŠA. Oh, don't be silly. It's only because of the day ahead.
When Lucy's about to take this… step.

VLADO. What? What are you thinking about? What if you'd
married someone else?

MAŠA. Not exactly.

VLADO. That 'non-aligned' chap? You thinking what would
have happened if he'd swept you off to Ethiopia?

MAŠA. The things that come into your head –

VLADO. I'd say the things that come into your head! You've
got me worried now.

MAŠA. Well, if you must know, there was a time when Stevo
asked me to go to Dubai with him.

VLADO. What? My Stevo?

MAŠA. Yes.

VLADO. When?

MAŠA. Before he left.

VLADO. What about Svetlana?

MAŠA. He said he'd leave her.

VLADO. I beg your pardon? My Stevo? (*Pause.*) Motherfucker.
Motherfucker!

    VLADO *gets out of bed, starts pacing.*

    That Serbian weasel! Brotherhood and unity my arse!

MAŠA. Calm down.

VLADO. 'Calm down'?! Maša, are you about to make some
sort of a confession? You know I don't enjoy impromptu
confessions.

MAŠA. Nothing happened! I never even liked him. It was just
his stupid idea.

VLADO. So why tell me this?

MAŠA. Because. So you knew. Other men noticed me.

VLADO. What?

MAŠA. Yes. It never occurred to you. That men could notice
me. You never thought of me that way.

VLADO. Nonsense.

MAŠA. Tell me one instance when you were jealous.

VLADO. Jealousy is nothing to be proud of.

MAŠA. Just tell me one time.

VLADO. There were plenty of times.

MAŠA. Name one.

    VLADO *ponders. He can't remember.*

    Like I wasn't even a woman.

VLADO. Well, Maša, you never complained. I mean, if you'd
said…

MAŠA. You could have asked.

VLADO. And what would you have said if I'd asked?

MAŠA *is silent*.

Say it now.

MAŠA. Something more. That marriage is more than just a double working shift. That you ask yourself, occasionally, what's going on with my wife? Does she need anything? Is she happy?

VLADO. Weren't you happy?

MAŠA. Ah, I don't know... what does it mean to be happy, anyway?

VLADO. Happy is what I've been with you. So I assumed that you have been happy with me.

Pause.

MAŠA. I haven't.

VLADO *stares at her, stunned. He huffs and puffs, lost for words.*

It's my own fault. I should have stood up for myself. Ever since I was a little girl. When Dad looked at me with that pent-up suspicion. When people whispered in the street when Karolina looked after me. Nobody explained there was file on her. For all I knew, it was because I was fat!

VLADO. Maša, what can I do?

MAŠA. Nothing. We are where we are. That's not the point. The point is I try to instil in our girls a sense of owning their destiny. This is how I make amends, to myself. And what do I get? Two people I don't understand. In a world I no longer understand. One of them I drove away –

VLADO. You did not!

MAŠA. With my overprotectiveness –

VLADO. Maša –

MAŠA. The other one has me perplexed every day. And this man...

VLADO. I said, didn't I say we should do something about that? When she first brought him round?

MAŠA. You said, Maša, you should talk to her. Do something about that.

VLADO (*quietly*). The idea deserves some credit.

MAŠA. The truth is, he confuses me. It's as if words don't mean the same any more. Trusting means stupid. Considerate means weak. Solidarity means you don't know how to look after yourself. We're so outdated we may as well be wearing a mullet.What we think is right he thinks is quaint and funny. And when she looks like she understands perfectly, I feel powerless against them.

VLADO. We always taught them about choice and free will.

MAŠA. My own lessons come back to bite me in the arse. And God only knows what is it that Alisa needs?

VLADO. I'd be happy if she found someone, albeit a woman.

VLADO *embraces* MAŠA *and cuddles up to her.*

MAŠA. There's yet another union looming over us. We were not brought up for uncertainty. There was a wonderful sense of certainty, do you remember?

VLADO. Maša, it will be all right.

MAŠA. You said that just before the war broke out.

VLADO *sighs, frustrated.*

VLADO. You know what, we lost Igor. In a way we lost Marko, too. Now, I'm not sure what we're supposed to measure ourselves against, but to all intents and purposes, we made it through, alive and reasonably well. I don't know how much time we have left. But I can't keep re-examining decisions. I am old. And I am tired. They understand life better than you or me. We have to let go. Maybe there is some unexpected happiness to be found in that.

She rests her head on him.

What do you think, we go to Dubai, after all?

MAŠA. Sure.

VLADO. I mean it. Go to Dubai, beat the shit out of Stevo. Over your honour. Would that make you happy?

MAŠA. Very.

VLADO. Listen. Fuck Dubai. But somewhere like that. Tunisia. Egypt. I bet you the prices have gone way down.

MAŠA. That's all I need: more of you, only with heat and sand.

VLADO. I'm serious. We marry Lucy off, pack Alisa off to a convent – and you and I go sailing down the Nile. To Luxor. And the Valley of the Kings.

MAŠA. All right.

They settle down to sleep.

VLADO. I'll ask you how you are and what you need every day.

MAŠA. Oh, dear.

VLADO. I'll get it all fixed. I hear you can organise everything through the internet. Let's just get through this day without drama and leave the rest to me.

Scene Thirteen

November, 2011.

Morning in the Kos household.

White-flower arrangements have been placed in the living room. The telly is on. On the telly we see an older KARL in an expensive suit, at a press conference.

KARL. It is clear by now that the Croatian people have developed a sophisticated sense for political thinking and have chosen the intelligent road to the future. The Croats have always felt a deep belonging to Europe – historical, political and geographical.

VLADO, *sixty-seven, wanders in, in his best suit, putting on his jacket. He stops in front of the telly, watching* KARL, *he does his belt up. The phone rings.*

I'm confident the referendum will show that the opportunity to shape our future in cooperation with other nations is something we have always had a desire for.

MAŠA, *sixty-six, rushes through the house, her hair done up, buzzing around with a million things on her mind. The phone is still ringing.*

MAŠA. Turn that man off, will you? The guests will be here any minute. And listen, keep an eye on how much you drink. You don't want to start going on about the partisans and Communists. You know they're not the right kind of people for that. Will someone answer the damn phone?

The ringing stops.

VLADO. Not that I ever get drunk, but if there's a day that calls for it...

MAŠA. Vlado...

VLADO. Come, give us a kiss.

MAŠA. Let go.

VLADO. Give us a kiss, right now!

He kisses her.

DUNJA, *sixty-three, enters, also in her best clothes, a cigarette in her hand. A white veil covers her face. The False Bride. A peculiar sight.* MAŠA *and* VLADO *look at her, lost for words. Absent-mindedly,* MAŠA *waves the smoke away.*

DUNJA. Does it look stupid?

ALISA *wanders in, wearing the same clothes as the night before.*

ALISA. Not as stupid as it probably feels.

DUNJA *flips the veil over her head, revealing her face.*

MAŠA. Alisa!

MAŠA *scans* ALISA. *The phone starts ringing again.*

You haven't changed since last night? What have you been doing?

ALISA. I couldn't sleep. I don't see how you could sleep.

MAŠA *clocks* VLADO. *The ringing continues.*

I was on the internet.

VLADO. Now, that's not sensible. How are you going to get through the day? Internet is not a toy.

ALISA. I was reading up, trying not to arrive at the wrong conclusion, get my facts straight and all that –

MAŠA. What facts?

ALISA. I've been questioning, all night I've been questioning my instincts and my, well, my right, to interfere as an outsider –

MAŠA. You're not an outsider –

ALISA. Thank you. But I am. I am a bit.

MAŠA. No, you absolutely are not. I would be heartbroken if you felt that – Lucija, will you answer the damn phone! Seriously!

She marches out to get the phone.

ALISA. And then last night – Marko said –

DUNJA. You saw Marko?

ALISA. Yes. Well… only briefly.

DUNJA. When?

ALISA. Late. Very late. I went to… enquire about the noise and then we got to talking and… (*Pausing.*) I really need Lucy to be here.

DUNJA. And what?

ALISA (*gathering courage*). Well –

LUCIJA *walks in in her white dress, looking like a Barbie doll.*

LUCIJA (*to* MAŠA *who is offstage*). Don't they have a GP-bloody-S? (*To the rest of them.*) The caterers are lost. Really. (*Realising she walked into something.*) What's going on?

MAŠA *re-enters.*

ALISA. Were our neighbours threatened into moving out? (*Beat.*) Anyone.

VLADO *sits down.*

LUCIJA. What do you think you are doing exactly?

ALISA. I'm sorry, I really am, but I can't not bring this up, I'm sorry –

LUCIJA. I can tell.

ALISA. Well?

LUCIJA. Well what?

ALISA. It's no secret, or at least not a very well-kept secret, that Damjan's business has been involved in a couple of contentious affairs.

She waves around some printouts.

LUCIJA. Every business in this country, at least every viable business has been involved in contentious affairs. That is how the world operates here.

DUNJA. That's how the world operates everywhere.

MAŠA. A lot of the stuff in the papers is just nonsense. He's taken them to court –

ALISA (*skimming through her printouts*)....privatised companies suddenly declaring bankruptcy, people losing jobs, you tend to trip over his name. Which makes the idea of threats sound... not implausible at all.

LUCIJA. So what exactly are you saying?

ALISA. Did Damjan force our neighbours to move?

Beat.

LUCIJA. He gave everyone a hefty compensation.

ALISA. But did they want to move?

LUCIJA. A moot point. If he hadn't offered to buy them out, they probably wouldn't have moved. But since he had –

ALISA. Okay, all right. Forget the papers. So let's put aside that we have no idea how exactly he has come to be so wonderfully well off –

LUCIJA. I'm sorry, did you want Damjan to present you with his books for inspection?

ALISA. You're all done up like horses on a parade and you just stand around and keep quiet while he buys the house and kicks people out?

LUCIJA. He has paid them compensation!

ALISA. He forced it on them!

LUCIJA. What proof have you got of that?

ALISA. Excuse me?

LUCIJA. Serious allegations like those require proof. More than mutterings of disgruntled neighbours.

ALISA. Serious allegations like those deserve to be investigated.

LUCIJA. How can you possibly be so opposed to us owning what belongs to us, something we have been a part of for a hundred years?

ALISA. It doesn't belong to us!

LUCIJA. Karolina said it did. If we hadn't all been so complacent, if we'd let her have her say in her will, maybe she would have explained!

MAŠA. Great-Grandma Monika said, when she was dying, she said we must hold on to it because it should be rightfully ours.

LUCIJA. There.

ALISA. There what? If it hadn't been for the Communists and their radical ideas on property, none of us would ever have had the opportunity to step inside it. Listen to yourself…

Great-Grandma Monika was barely more than a slave in this house and Grandma Rose sure as hell would not stand for buying properties and turning people out!

DUNJA. You know what happens if it turns out that somewhere in Argentina, Karolina has some relatives who decide to rock up here and claim old Amruš's inheritance?

ALISA (*to* DUNJA). I'm surprised at you, Dunja. In the veil. You never used to have time for bullies.

DUNJA. Their tactics have changed.

LUCIJA. Excuse me?

ALISA (*to* LUCIJA). So let's assume, for the sake of the argument, that private property is indeed the key to our identity –

LUCIJA. Please, allow me to dim the lights in the audience first –

ALISA (*to* LUCIJA). How is the house going to be ours? A total bloody stranger is buying our house and you are rolling out the red carpet for him.

LUCIJA. He's not a stranger. He's going to be one of us. We are about to get married!

ALISA. He is never going to be one of us. He's one of them. He's like Karolina's father. He's like Karl. Not like us –

LUCIJA. He is not like Karl. Fuck you. Fuck you, Alisa. How dare you say that?

ALISA. The Horaks received threats.

LUCIJA. The Horaks deserve threats. They made our lives hell for decades.

ALISA. Marko said that it was made clear to him, very early on in the negotiations that turning the offer down would not be an option.

LUCIJA. Marko is a frustrated middle-aged mamma's boy who's fucked off with everyone who did well in the aftermath.

VLADO. I will not have you belittling Marko –

ALISA. Because the aftermath proved incredibly lucrative for some –

VLADO. The hubris of the successful, I will not stand for it. Marko has done a great deal of good –

LUCIJA. So has Damjan! Worked hard, started from nothing, done well. Wants to marry, start a family, provide for them, why is he being subjected to so much suspicion and mistrust –

DUNJA. He is actually being bestowed quite an amount of trust –

ALISA. No one has even asked him the question –

VLADO. I asked the question. (*Beat.*) I asked Damjan. If it was true. About the threats.

LUCIJA. What did you do?

VLADO. All this letting-go business, well, that's just crock.

LUCIJA. Dad?

VLADO. We talked about it, Mum and myself and… Dunja and we decided we can't ignore what is being said. Even if in the form of mutterings. So I asked him.

LUCIJA. You went behind my back –

VLADO. Yes. I did. I felt I needed to do it face to face.

ALISA. And?

VLADO. And he swore, he gave me his word it was not true.

ALISA. And?

VLADO. What do you mean?

ALISA. That's all? He gave you his word?

VLADO. Doesn't a man's word count for anything any more?

ALISA. 'A man's word'? You're a historian! When did a man's word count for anything? How can you just roll over and let this happen? Did you have a stroke that we all missed?

MAŠA. Alisa! Show some respect!

ALISA. It's because I respect him I expect more from him!

VLADO. What is it you expect? What can I do? Except confront him? And then take his word? Pursue it and drive a wedge between us and Lucy? What if she picks him and leaves? What happens then? We are left here at the end of our days, without you both. You think your mum would survive that?

MAŠA. Vlado…

VLADO. Well, yes. It's a consideration. I have spent my life trying to do the right thing and I have more than once hurt my family whilst staying true to my principles. So. I have decided to take the man's word for it. Because in my world, albeit an outdated, senile world of small strokes, that still counts for something.

ALISA. Great. Well, that settles it then. (*Raises her hand in salutation.*) Pioneer's honour.

MAŠA *breaks down in tears.*

Mum. Oh, God. Mum, please don't cry.

They gather around her.

LUCIJA. Great.

ALISA. Don't put this on me. I'm not the one who made her cry. You made her cry if anyone –

DUNJA. Shut up, both of you. Maša, darling. Mashenka.

MAŠA. I'm okay. I don't know what came over me. I'm okay.

She takes a moment, breathing deeply. Everyone watches her. LUCIJA undoes her corset a little, allowing her to breathe more easily. She paces up and down. ALISA gazes at her.

I do really wonder whether a small stroke would not be a blessing.

It hasn't been easy to come to terms with having Damjan for a son-in-law.

LUCIJA. Perfect timing, Mum.

MAŠA. But we try. To keep an open mind. Which is hard at our age.

Every morning I wake up I feel the open mind has shrunk a little more. And still, we try. To weigh things out. To be fair to him and Lucy. Not let prejudice cloud our judgement. Stay objective... One way or another this family has lived in this house for a hundred years. Perhaps in this day and age we must let those who understand the way the world works better, take the helm. Because sticking to our principles has cost us dearly in the past. We barely made it through. And now I fear, we might just sink.

ALISA. You have put your fate in the hands of someone who has little regard for others and no concept of a hundred-year-long continuity. Because, objectively speaking, a hundred years the ivy's been wrapping itself around this house and now he has stripped it down. The house looks bare, robbed of its... It looks violated. Where the fuck is the ivy?

LUCIJA. The ivy?!

MAŠA. Well, the refurbishment... it had to be taken down...

LUCIJA. The ivy?! You know what, Alice in fucking Wonderland. That's correct. The house needs refurbishment. Because for something like seventy years nobody could afford it. So the ivy had to go. I'm sorry if that offends your sensibilities when you come home once a year. I made Damjan buy the house. You think that would have been his first choice? Live with all of you? But I persuaded him, so that this amazing house in prime location containing three elderly families hardly making ends meet did not become a target for someone less sentimental. As is often the case nowadays in this beautiful country.

ALISA. And is the case for our neighbours.

LUCIJA. They were all paid out! You have no idea how things work here! You can't get an ingrown hair looked at without bribing someone. Since Mum retired, these two poor old bastards can't make the utility bills every month. Dunja sits here like a church mouse after ten years in court with a wife-beater. Ten years. Before losing the case. But when I said we should send a couple of guys over to Karl's for a little chat, my God, the outrage! We're not going down that route. We'll rely on the courts. The law is on our side. Yeah. Congratulations. Well, finally she will have protection.

Dad still plays the lottery every week. Mum goes on about how things used to be better. 'We didn't have much but we felt safe.' Which is a curious concept as everyone ended up slaughtering each other.

Now we're going to join the EU and it's all going to change again. A hundred years of turmoil. And back to being a colony. Cheers.

But I'm not letting this place go. Because of our history and our life here, which was largely happy, I won't let someone buy it and kick *them* out and turn it into a spa. Because I'm fucking sentimental. And as for you – if I remember correctly, last time I came to visit, your landlady couldn't for the life of her remember if Croatia was in Russia or the other way around and despite your PhD in things she can't pronounce, when you had three girlfriends over from Croatia she was this close to calling a raid on you. Because, what do you call four Croatian women in one flat? A brothel, obviously. So when you come back, I'll have to carry you all because I was the only one smart enough to adapt. I know it comes as a surprise to everyone that I'm the one to step up, but hey, life is full of surprises!

A stunned silence.

And the house is going to be ours. It's in my name. Do you think I'm stupid?

Beat.

ALISA. He agreed?

LUCIJA. Luckily it bodes well if the taxman ever pays a visit.

Silence. VLADO *has sat down on the chair, looking completely worn-out.* DUNJA *lights a cigarette.*

ALISA. This is wrong, Lucija. It's wrong.

LUCIJA. Alisa… (*Pause.*) You need to scrub up. (*Pointing to her appearance.*) This is unacceptable. Mum, you need to get me some wet wipes, I am sweating like a pig. Dunja, you need to call the caterers and tell them if they're not here in five minutes, they needn't bother coming and they can deal with Damjan later. Dad, you might want to take a Xanax cos we don't want you getting confrontational at church. Also, someone needs to go over 'Holy Father' with me – it's going to be embarrassing if I get it wrong. And let's see if we can all work up a smile. This is the happiest day of my fucking life.

Loud folk music is heard from the street. At first a faint sound far away and then coming closer and closer. The groom, followed by the band, is on his way.

The Kos family stand around the room, as if frozen.

Scene Fourteen

November, 1945.

KAROLINA's *bedroom.*

MONIKA, *forty-five, sits in the chair next to* KAROLINA, *forty-seven.*

MONIKA. He said things to me I never heard anyone say before. It was late. He came into the kitchen. He said his name was Sebastian. He said, 'I am Karolina's brother.' I said, 'I know.' I said, Miss Karolina talked about him often. He wanted some hot milk. He said the thing he could never find in England was milk that tasted the same like milk from our cows. I thought that was funny. Aren't cows the same everywhere? He had a packet of cigarettes. With beautiful golden lettering. He asked me if I wanted one. 'I don't smoke,' I said.

Music is heard from the garden. A wedding band. ALISA. *thirty-six, comes into the bedroom and starts packing her suitcase.*

He said the world was a deeply disappointing place. What is a man to do who comes from a monarchy, which is coming to an end, who belongs to a nation of underdogs and lives in a country where he will always be second class. He said 'I don't belong there, I come back and I don't belong here.' He said he wished he was like his sister. Who still believes that life, her wonderful, exciting life will begin one day when she breaks free. Only she has no idea one can never break free. Maybe a simpler life is what we should all be striving for. Out here in our wonderful country. Grow crops, drink the milk and make love. Here where the air is clean and the people are good.

He said I was very beautiful. He said my head was not poisoned by thoughts, these thoughts, which become like tentacles that reach in all directions and infect your whole body with poison. These thoughts about how terrible the world is and how evil men are. I know none of that. My eyes are kind and pure. He asked my name. 'Monika,' I said. 'Monika. Monika. Monika. I shall carry your name with me as a memory of this encounter with the very essence of what's good and pure about us.' And he said, 'Do you know you are the most noble of creatures?' 'The reverend says a woman is made of a man's rib,' I said. 'Isn't a rib a finer material than mud and dust, which Adam was made of? First he made many creatures of the sea. And then of the earth. Four-legged and crawling creatures, much lesser than a human being. Then he made a human being, a creature superior to all before – a man. But only then, he made a woman, the most perfect creature thus far. And only when he made a woman, he could rest.'

And he looked into my eyes. 'Who knows,' he said, 'what life has in store for us? I sometimes still find hope in that.'

No one, no one has ever looked into my eyes like that before. I have never been looked at like that before. He looked at me like I was an amazing jewel. And then he kissed me.

Young ALISA *and* MARKO *kiss in the snow.*

Old KAROLINA *twirls in her wheelchair alone. The snow falls on her.*

LUCIJA *in her glamorous, white ball gown dances with* VLADO.

DUNJA *dances with* IGOR.

ROSE *dances with* ALEKSANDAR.

MAŠA *dances with* VLADO.

ALISA *stands in front of the house. She picks up the suitcase and leaves.*

End of play.

Guide to Pronunciation

Most words are pronounced with the emphasis on the first syllable.

Amruš	Amroosh
Damjan	Damyan
Dunja	Dunya
Karlovac	Karlovatz
Lucija	Lutzia
Maljević	Malyevich
Marić	Marich
Milošević	Miloshevich
Pavelić	Pavelich
Račan	Rachan
Tuđman	Tudjman
Ustaše	Ustashe
Vrapče	Vrapche